Working with Difficult PEOPLE

Working Difficult *with* PEOPLE

NICHOLAS MINSHALL

WORKING WITH DIFFICULT PEOPLE

Copyright © 2019 by Nicholas Minshall

First Edition: April 2019

ISBN-10: 1092461027
ISBN-13: 978-1092461023

Part I

Identifying Difficult People

Almost everyone has encountered difficult people in the workplace. Difficult people can exhibit different behaviors, such as rudeness, yelling, gossiping, ignoring, or harassing. Being able to deal with these people can make for a less stressful and more productive work environment.

1

Common Types of Difficult People

To effectively deal with difficult people, you first need to be able to identify the type of difficult person you're dealing with. Then you can have a better understanding of the person's motivations. This will enable you to determine how best to deal with their behavior.

Identify difficult people

Difficult people can exhibit different behaviors. However, they can be categorized into a few common types. Think about some difficult people you've encountered. Perhaps someone who complained all the time. Or someone who seemed to be out only for themselves.

By being able to identify the type of difficult person you're dealing with, you can better prepare a strategy to use to deal with that person.

Understand motivations

Difficult people are motivated by many things. One person might be motivated by a need for attention. Another might be motivated by a fear of failure.

By understanding what motivates difficult people to act the way they do, you'll be in a better position to begin to be able to deal with them.

2

Recognizing Difficult People

Difficult people are everywhere. Can you think of a difficult person you've encountered in the workplace? Perhaps a coworker who complains constantly? Or somebody who's never able to meet a deadline?

Difficult people cause all kinds of problems in the workplace and make life miserable for their coworkers.

For example, a person who misses deadlines can cause coworkers who are forced to pick up the slack to become resentful. Likewise, a person who constantly complains can lower morale in the workplace.

Being able to deal with a difficult person is a skill that can serve you well in the workplace and can help you avoid or overcome awkward situations.

If you can identify what types of difficult people you're dealing with, you can better determine what motivates them to behave the way they do. Once you know the motivation for their behavior, you can understand how to deal with and or avoid the issues they cause. However, just because you see someone as difficult doesn't mean that person necessarily is.

It's important to understand these differences and consider them before labeling someone as "difficult." What may seem offensive to one person may seem completely normal to a person from a different cultural background.

Identifying Difficult People

For example, one person may see no problem with addressing a superior by the person's first name.

However, someone from a different cultural background may see this as a sign of disrespect.

Reflect

Think about people you've encountered at work who you felt were difficult. What could have influenced their behavior to cause you to see them that way?

Have you ever stopped to think that you could be the one being difficult? If you think about it, you can probably think of times when your behavior has caused problems for someone else.

Before you can think about a plan for dealing with someone who you feel is being difficult, you should look at your own behavior to see if it could be something you did that's causing the problem.

It may be a good idea to talk over the situation with someone you trust, such as a coworker, friend, or family member. This person may be able to help you determine whether it's your behavior that needs to change.

For the most part, people themselves aren't really "difficult." However, they do exhibit difficult behaviors. It's these behaviors that cause negative reactions from others. Some examples of the types of behaviors that can cause problems at work include being negative or disruptive, poor attendance, a lack of focus, or an unwillingness to change.

But what can cause people to exhibit difficult behavior? It may be the environment they're living or working in. Or they may be under a lot of pressure and feeling the effects of stress.

It's important to examine the person's behavior over a period of time. Does this person act this way all the time, or is this behavior new? If the behavior is out of the ordinary, the person may simply be having a bad day.

Difficult behavior needs to be dealt with in a timely fashion. If allowed to continue, it can get worse over time. People who feel that their behavior helps them get what they want have little incentive to change.

M argaret and Rudy have worked together for years. They've always worked well together and gotten along.

Last week, Margaret asked Rudy for advice on a project she was working on. Rudy responded angrily that he had enough on his own plate without having to do her work too. Because they've always bounced ideas off each other in the past, Margaret was surprised by Rudy's reaction.

Although her first reaction was to get angry herself, Margaret decided to talk to Rudy to see if everything was okay. Rudy revealed that he was under an unusual amount of stress because of an ill family member. By dealing with the situation, Margaret ensured things didn't escalate or affect their working relationship.

3

Types of Difficult People

Most difficult people that you'll encounter in the workplace can be divided into five general types: aggressive, negative, procrastinator, manipulative, and self-serving.

Each type of difficult person exhibits different behavior that requires a different approach.

Aggressive

Aggressive people tend to be rude and intimidating, trying to control others by behaving like bullies on a playground. They may use tactics such as yelling and threatening to frighten coworkers.

Or, in the case of passive-aggressive people, they may try to control you by dropping hints to make you feel sorry for them, rather than just asking you directly for help. For example, they may say something like, "I hope I can finish this project tonight. I'm not feeling well and I may not be in tomorrow," rather than just asking if you could help them finish the project.

In a worst-case scenario, aggressive behavior in the workplace can lead to violence. Consider the example of Megan, a call center supervisor who's in charge of a small group of agents. She holds team meetings once a week to discuss any issues with her agents.

During these meetings, she brings up any mistakes she sees being made by agents. She makes sure to use the names of these employees in front of the whole group, belittling them and calling them names.

Megan feels that if she embarrasses these employees, they won't make the same mistake again. That may be, but Megan's group has the highest absenteeism and turn-over rates in the call center.

Negative

Negative people complain about everything but never have suggestions for how to improve anything. They only seem to be happy when they're spreading misery to everyone else.

Negative people keep their coworkers from getting their work done by constantly distracting them. They also bring the people around them down.

Coworkers may start to ignore negative people, which can lead to another problem. On the rare occasion that the negative people really do have something that needs to be brought to their coworkers' attention, chances are nobody will be listening.

For example, Tyson spends his coffee and lunch breaks complaining to his coworkers about pretty much everything. His boss doesn't understand how hard he works. He doesn't make enough money. He gets passed over for every promotion. Even the weather never seems to suit him.

If anybody tries to steer the conversation in another direction, Tyson interrupts to bring the topic back to

Identifying Difficult People

him and his problems. Whatever anybody else is talking about, he finds a way to see something negative about it.

Tyson's coworkers will do just about anything to avoid him. When he walks into the break room, everyone else suddenly decides it's time to get back to work. But they can't get away that easily. Tyson follows his coworkers back to their desks to complain some more, distracting them from their work.

Procrastinator

Procrastinators find reasons to put off doing their tasks. They often have trouble getting started and spend time thinking of excuses for why they can't get their work done.

Procrastinators are often afraid of failure. In their minds, missing a deadline is better than submitting poorly done work. Procrastinators will often have trouble meeting deadlines and require more time to complete a task than their coworkers.

In cases where production depends on a number of tasks being completed by different people, a procrastinator can throw everything off. Coworkers may be forced to pick up the slack and will eventually become resentful.

For example, Joel knows his manager is waiting for a report that she asked him to prepare last week. He knows he needs to get it done soon, as she'll be looking for it. The truth is, Joel hasn't even started the report yet. He's not sure what he needs to do, and he doesn't want to ask his manager because he doesn't want to admit he hasn't started.

Joel decides he'd better get started. But then one of his coworkers asks if Joel has time to help out with something. Joel decides he should help his coworker first, and then he can get started on the report.

After helping his coworker, Joel is ready to start the report. Then he remembers something else he should do.

By the end of the day, he still hasn't started the report. "That's okay" he thinks. "I'll get it done tomorrow."

The next day, Joel's manager asks about the report. He tells her that it's almost done, and that he just needs a few more days.

Manipulative

Manipulative people use their charms to coax and maneuver their coworkers to suit their own needs. Manipulators are self-centered and don't care about anyone else's wants or needs. They enjoy being the center of attention – it doesn't matter to them how they get there.

When manipulators run into people who don't give them the answers they want, they often turn to threats to get their way. For example, a manipulator who feels secure in the workplace may threaten to quit if the boss won't give her what she wants.

Manipulators see no problem with using whatever tactics they deem necessary to get their coworkers to

Identifying Difficult People

help them out. However, they would seldom put themselves out to help someone else.

For example, Omar works for a construction company. When he's given a task that he doesn't want to do, he usually convinces one of his coworkers to do it for him instead.

His boss asks him to work on the roof of the building, but Omar would rather stay on the ground and interact with people walking by.

Omar asks his boss to get someone else to do the work on the roof. He says he hurt his leg and doesn't feel comfortable climbing the ladder to get to the roof.

Omar makes a big deal about it in front of his coworkers. He declares he is more than capable of doing his job on the ground floor. Omar says that it's unfair of his boss to refuse to accommodate him.

His boss, who doesn't want to look like the bad guy, asks another worker to take Omar's place on the roof. Omar is pleased with himself. The next time a situation arises, Omar will have another excuse ready to get his way.

Self-serving

Self-serving people believe in getting something for nothing. They don't see value in achieving things through hard work.

They tend to believe that what they feel is best for them is really the fair and moral choice.

At Maureen's workplace, there's a group that organizes weekly luncheons, with all proceeds going to charity. Every week, Maureen has an excuse for not going. She forgot her wallet or her mortgage payment is due that week and she can't afford to be spending any extra money.

A few times a year, the same group has a free luncheon to thank everyone for all their contributions. Maureen always attends the free luncheons and sees nothing wrong with it.

Sometimes, you might think people are being difficult when they really aren't. Saying or doing something you don't like doesn't necessarily make a person difficult.

For example, a boss may need to give corrective feedback to an employee. The employee might be upset about the feedback, but the boss isn't being difficult. She's just doing her job.

4

Causes of Difficult Behavior

When a person acts disruptively in the workplace, coworkers are often quick to label that person as difficult.

In most cases, it's not people that are difficult, but rather their behavior. But why would someone choose to behave in a difficult way? People will often use difficult behavior if, in the past, it's helped them get what they want or need. It's easier to understand difficult people if you can identify the reasons behind their behavior.

The difficult people in your office probably don't see themselves as difficult. In fact, they probably think you're the difficult one. After all, you're what's standing between them and what they want.

But if you change your reaction to reflect their behavior types, they may start to think of you as being more reasonable, and in turn, change their reactions and behavior. Realizing that changing your behavior can help to change theirs can help you more easily combat difficult behavior.

In order to deal with a person's difficult behavior, it helps to understand what the person wants and needs. However, identifying someone's wants and needs may not always be possible. Identifying intent, or what the person hopes to accomplish with his behavior, can be easier.

If you have a difficult relationship with a coworker, it may be helpful to ask the person's opinion about why the relationship is difficult. Doing this helps to create a feeling of being in control.

If you choose this approach, it's important to remember that you may not always like what you hear. You need to be able to really listen without taking it personally. By listening to the words and not just reacting, you may find clues to your coworker's motivations and needs.

Reflect

Think about somebody you've encountered in the workplace whose behavior you would classify as difficult. What do you think may have been the cause of this person's behavior?

If somebody has been rewarded for difficult behavior in the past by having his needs met, he has no incentive to change. For example, if every time a coworker interrupts you, you stop what you're doing to listen, the coworker will probably continue to behave this way.

Dealing with the difficult behavior of others isn't easy, and you shouldn't expect instant results. Changing someone's behavior takes time.

Difficult behavior can also be caused by deeper issues. Some of these issues include lack of experience, being stuck in the past, and having low self-esteem. Understanding why difficult people behave the way they do can help you develop a strategy to deal with the issues they cause.

Dysfunctional family

People who grow up with a lack of experience in different social settings may have never learned the basic social skills to enable them to interact appropriately with others.

For example, someone who wasn't given any privacy while growing up may become an adult who sees nothing wrong with intruding into everyone else's personal lives. This person doesn't understand or respect other people's need for privacy.

Stuck in the past

People who are stuck in the past may exhibit difficult behavior because they relate to people in the present as though they were a specific person who caused them grief in the past.

For instance, someone who was treated abusively or unfairly by a previous boss may feel anger toward a new boss because of their unresolved anger. The person behaves badly toward the new boss because, in that person's eyes, the new boss represents someone from the past who caused him pain.

Low self-esteem

People with low self-esteem will often use difficult behavior, such as being demanding or offensive, to keep others at a distance. They do this to protect their own fragile sense of self.

As an example, they may have been teased or bullied as children and have learned to respond to others in the same manner.

5

Understanding Motivations

Understanding some of the common causes of difficult behavior is a good starting point. However, understanding what motivates someone to behave in a certain way will equip you to develop a strategy to effectively deal with that person's behavior.

Some common types of difficult behavior you may encounter in the workplace are controlling, perfectionist, approval-seeking, and attention-getting. Each type of behavior has a different motivation and requires a different approach.

Controlling

Megan is a call center supervisor who meets with each of her agents individually every month to discuss performance. Megan's biggest complaint with her agents is that they take too long on each call.

She tells the agents that they need to use whatever means necessary to finish the call as soon as possible and move on to the next one.

If Megan notices an agent has been on a call for what she thinks is too long, she'll often stand over him while he's talking, giving him disapproving looks while pointing at her watch.

Megan is motivated to get the job done quickly to keep costs down. This causes her to exhibit controlling behavior. Controlling behavior is also a type of aggressive behavior.

What Megan needs to understand is that not all calls can be handled that quickly. If customers don't feel that situations are resolved, they may call back repeatedly until they're satisfied.

Megan's agents may need to explain that sometimes it takes time to get to the root of a customer's problem. Megan needs to understand that by taking a little extra time to resolve issues on the first call, her agents are actually cutting back on the number of callbacks and dissatisfied customers. And this saves the company money in the long run.

Perfectionist

Joel is trying to get his report finished and asks a coworker for help. But for every suggestion his coworker makes, Joel finds something wrong with it.

"What if that's not exactly what the boss wants?" he thinks. Joel is more afraid of doing something wrong than he is of angering his boss by missing another deadline.

Joel has started his report a number of times. He gets so far, decides he can do better, and starts over. At this rate, he may never get it done.

Joel is motivated by a need to get the job done right, which is causing him to behave like a perfectionist. Perfectionists can often be indecisive and overly critical. This is a type of procrastination.

This type of behavior may be brought on by Joel's need for approval. However, his behavior can really slow down a project. Because he doesn't feel like what he's done is good enough, he's unable to move on to the next step.

To counteract this behavior, Joel's boss needs to provide him with lots of support and reassurance. Joel's boss needs to make him understand that being able to get a job done well and on time is more important than spending so much time on every little detail.

Approval-seeking

Cindy, a law firm receptionist, has a problem saying no to her coworkers. One coworker, Neil, is constantly late for work and expects Cindy to cover his phone for him. Cindy has told Neil she can't keep covering for him, but she continues to do it anyway.

Another coworker is always asking Cindy to help out with typing and filing. Cindy doesn't have time, but says it's no problem, because she doesn't want to be thought of as difficult. She wants her coworkers to like her.

Cindy is having a hard time keeping up at the office, but doesn't want her coworkers to think less of her. But if Cindy is unable to complete all the work she's taken on, somebody will end up angry with her.

Cindy is motivated by the need to get along and belong and is exhibiting approval-seeking behavior. She doesn't want to say no to anyone, and will agree to all requests. This may often result in Cindy not being able to do any of her work effectively. Approval-seeking behavior is a type of negative behavior.

Cindy wants to be thought of as the "nice" person, always agreeable and willing to help out. That's why she hasn't been able to stick to her decision to not cover for her coworker.

Cindy needs to understand that it's not always possible to please everybody. And, by trying to do just that, she isn't able to do her job effectively and risks making people angry at her. Cindy's boss may help her by taking on the role of the "bad guy" and telling

Cindy's coworkers not to ask her for help with their work.

Attention-getting

Maureen likes to be the center of attention at work. During a staff meeting, after the boss is done explaining a new project, she asks if anyone has any questions. One employee raises his hand and asks a question. Maureen immediately interrupts so she can let everyone know what she thinks the answer is.

Her boss then says that she's right, and Maureen is pleased with herself. Later that day, she drops by her boss's office to discuss another idea for the project. Her boss tells her that he's busy at the moment and asks if it can wait. She comes in anyway, saying it will only take a minute. Her boss begrudgingly puts his work aside for the moment to listen to her.

A few hours later, Maureen is back in her boss's office to discuss some more ideas. Her boss is starting to get annoyed, because she's making it difficult for him to get his own work done.

Maureen is motivated by the need to be appreciated and is displaying attention-getting behavior. This is a type of self-serving behavior.

She has no problem interrupting others' work by calling or stopping by their offices constantly. She's often seen as a pest by her boss and coworkers.

To help mitigate this difficult behavior, Maureen's boss needs to acknowledge her and let her know she is appreciated. Once Maureen gains the approval she's seeking, the situation should start to improve.

6

Dealing with Difficult People

It would be great if there was one easy answer when it comes to dealing with difficult people. But there isn't. You'll need to deal with each difficult person you encounter individually.

Sometimes, a difficult person has traits from multiple types of difficult behavior. For example, someone may exhibit traits of a negative person, but at times also be aggressive or manipulative. But you don't need to feel overwhelmed by all the combinations of behavior you might encounter. Even though the answers for each difficult person's behavior are different, the methods of finding those answers are the same.

One thing to keep in mind is that change must come from your side. Remember, you're the one who thinks there's a problem. You're the one who's distressed by the situation, and the person causing the distress isn't likely to just go away.

You also need to realize that the difficult person won't likely change. Difficult people seldom think of themselves as difficult, so there's no incentive for them to change their behavior.

Realizing that the person causing you problems isn't going away and isn't going to change, it's up to you to obtain a better understanding of the behavior that's causing you distress.

It's not easy to react in the best way when confronted with a difficult person. It's tough to stay calm when somebody's pushing your buttons. You don't want to lose your self-control and say or do something that ends up making the situation worse.

To deal with a difficult person effectively, you need to prepare yourself before the encounter. If you're prepared, it'll make it easier to remain on track and focused on dealing with the problem.

Reflect

What ways can you think of to prepare yourself for an encounter with a difficult person?

Analyzing the situation will better prepare you for an encounter with a difficult person. Try to describe the behavior of the difficult person. What is it specifically about that person's behavior that's causing problems? Is there anything about your behavior that could possibly be making things worse?

Try to think about the motivations behind the person's behavior. Ask yourself if there's anything you can do to reduce the effect of the behavior.

The second action you can take is role-playing the situation. Ask someone to play the part of the difficult person. This will give you a chance to rehearse the encounter with the difficult person and how you'll respond to the difficult behavior.

It may also be beneficial to switch roles and play the difficult person yourself, giving you a chance to see how somebody else would deal with the situation.

Practice the role-playing until you feel comfortable with your response. The more you rehearse the encounter, the more likely you'll be to stand up to the behavior of the difficult person. And you'll be less likely to respond inappropriately when the encounter happens for real.

7

Steps for Success

When you encounter a difficult person, there are some actions you should avoid. For example, you shouldn't ignore the problem behavior, respond to the behavior in kind, blame the person instead of problem solving, or try to psychoanalyze the person.

The first action you need to avoid is ignoring the problem behavior. Ignoring it won't make it go away. In fact, it may even get worse, which will only cause bigger problems in the long run. In some cases, if others see you ignoring the bad behavior, they might see it as a sign that it's okay to behave that way. They may end up adopting the bad behavior themselves.

The second action to avoid is responding in kind. Responding in kind to someone's difficult behavior won't solve the problem, only complicate it. It won't make you feel any better, and it'll probably make you feel angrier and less in control of the situation.

The third action to avoid is blaming the person instead of problem solving. Blaming the person won't change the situation. Blaming other people is just a way to punish them. Blame will only lead to conflict and put more distance between you and the other person.

The last action to avoid is psychoanalyzing the person. When you try to understand people's motivations for difficult behavior, you may be tempted to psychoanalyze them. For example, you might think your difficult coworker didn't get enough attention as a child or acts out because of a need to control others.

But whether your psychoanalysis is correct or not won't make much difference in your relationship with the difficult person. Instead of spending too much time trying to figure out why someone is the way he is, it is better to accept it and work from there.

Reflect

Think about an encounter you've had with a difficult person where you reacted by ignoring the behavior, blaming the person, or responding in kind. What could you have done instead?

When you encounter a difficult person, there are three steps you should take – perhaps your answer included some of them. You need to do a reality check to determine whether there's really a problem. If there is and you need to confront the person, be sure to listen carefully and always give feedback.

First, you need to do a reality check. To do a reality check, ask yourself whether the difficult person's behavior is causing problems in performance. If the answer is no, what will happen if you leave the situation alone? Will it get worse? If the behavior isn't impacting performance and won't get worse if left alone, it may make sense to do nothing.

But don't just think about how the person's behavior impacts you. It's just as important to consider how others in the workplace are affected. Do others feel the same way you do? Is their performance being affected?

Next, you need to listen carefully. Listening is a valuable skill to help you prevent and resolve conflict. During an encounter with a difficult person, it's important that you listen carefully to that person. By listening, you provide the person with validation and empathy.

Ask questions that summarize what the person is saying, and rephrase what you're hearing to show that you understand. This way, you can avoid misunderstandings that could escalate the situation.

And last, make sure you give feedback. In many cases, the difficult person may not be aware that his behavior is causing problems. Giving timely feedback about the difficult behavior can help avoid misunderstandings. It can also help to clarify expectations.

When giving feedback to someone about behavior, use "I" statements. For example, if a coworker constantly interrupts you while you're working, don't say "Your constant interruptions are annoying me and you're making it impossible for me to get my work done". Instead, say something like "I feel frustrated when I'm interrupted because it's difficult for me to pick up where I left off."

Make sure that you let the person know what's expected. Set clear guidelines for what behavior is inappropriate – and why – and how it should change.

When interacting with a difficult person, it's important that you remember to stay calm. Getting angry or excited or losing your self-control will only make the situation worse. Slow down and resist the urge to react negatively. Think before you speak. By staying calm, you remain in control and avoid knee-jerk reactions. Remember that decisions made in the heat of the moment aren't usually good ones.

Stay focused on the behavior and not on the person. If you can separate the two, you can be hard on the behavior while being soft on the person. First, you must try to understand the nature of the problem. What's the specific behavior that's unacceptable? How often and with whom does it occur?

Talk to the difficult person. Explain clearly what behavior is difficult and why it's a concern. Stick to the facts and avoid offering your opinion of why the person acts the way she does. And listen to what she has to say. Show empathy and understanding.

Clearly state the change in behavior that you're seeking. However, keep an open mind about changing the goal if it's appropriate.

C indy and Neil work as receptionists at a law firm. Neil has a bad habit of being late for work. Whenever Neil is late, Cindy always covers for him, making sure his phones are answered. It used to be an occasional thing, but lately, it's happening two or three times a week.

Cindy knows she should say something to Neil, but she figures it's easier to just cover for him. But Neil is self-serving. He doesn't care about putting someone else out if it benefits him. And he tends to get upset if someone confronts him about it.

Recently, Cindy's boss told her he's been receiving a lot of complaints from clients, and that it's often impossible to get through to the office by phone. Cindy figures if she lets things continue the way they have been, she and Neil will both get in trouble with the boss.

Cindy realizes now that Neil's behavior isn't just an inconvenience, but is starting to cause problems for the company. She comes to the conclusion that she needs to speak with him about his tardiness. Follow along as Cindy confronts Neil during their coffee break.

<u>Cindy:</u>　　Neil, there's something I need to talk to you about. It's becoming too difficult for me to cover all of the calls in the morning by myself. I need you to start being on time in the morning.
Cindy sounds calm.

<u>Neil:</u> I'm sorry that I inconvenienced you, but I've had a very difficult morning. The car wouldn't start, the

Identifying Difficult People

babysitter was late, and traffic was horrible. I didn't realize it was that big a deal.
Neil sounds annoyed.

<u>Cindy:</u>   I'm sorry to hear you're having such a rough morning. I don't mind helping out now and then, but this is the third time you've been late this week. I've been getting complaints about calls not being answered, and I'm afraid that I'm not going to be able to cover for you anymore.
Cindy sounds calm.

<u>Neil:</u> You have no idea how hard my life is! Your life is easy compared to mine. You live a block away from the office. And your kids are in school, so you don't have to depend on a babysitter.
Neil sounds angry and resentful.

<u>Cindy:</u>   I understand you're having difficulties. Unfortunately, I just can't keep up with the workload when I'm the only one here. It's much easier when you're here on time. Is your babysitter late often? I can give you the number of one that I use. She's very dependable, and great with kids. And I think she's free during the day.
Cindy sounds helpful.

<u>Neil:</u> Thanks, Cindy. My babysitter has been showing up late a lot. I've been thinking about finding someone else, but I didn't know where to start. I'm sorry about putting you in a difficult situation in the mornings. I'll try harder to be on time from now on.

Neil sounds calm and grateful.

Cindy: You're welcome. I'll let her know to expect your call. I'm glad we had this talk.

Cindy followed the steps for dealing effectively with a difficult person. By performing a reality check, she realized that Neil's behavior was a problem that needed to be addressed.

Cindy listened to what Neil had to say. She was empathetic and understanding. When Neil became defensive and angry, Cindy started feeling angry too. But if she had given in to that feeling and told Neil how inconsiderate he was, the situation would probably have escalated. Instead, Cindy remained calm and stuck to the facts. She focused on the problem and tried to find a way to resolve it.

Cindy gave feedback. She let Neil know exactly what the problem was and what behavior needed to change. And she focused on Neil's behavior – his frequent lateness – instead of on Neil. Once Neil became aware of the problems he was causing, he agreed to make an effort to show up on time.

Cindy was able to solve her problem with Neil, but things don't always work out that easily. What if Neil had continued to show up late for work? What could Cindy have done then? If Cindy was in a position of authority over Neil, she may have been able to use performance management techniques to resolve the situation. But Cindy and Neil both have the same position within the company.

If talking with the difficult person doesn't have any effect, you can try getting a third person involved. For example, Cindy could have gotten another coworker to talk with Neil as well. Being confronted by a third person about his behavior may have been enough to make Neil realize that he couldn't continue to be late every day.

And, if all else fails, you can get someone in a position of authority to help out. If Cindy had been unable to reach a solution with Neil, then, as a last resort, she could have spoken with their supervisor about the problem. The supervisor could then take appropriate steps to correct Neil's behavior.

Part II

You Can't Change Them

There are difficult people in all walks of life. If you have to work with people you find difficult, it's best to learn how to respond and relate to them better instead of trying to change them. By learning about the importance of becoming self-aware and building emotional intelligence when dealing with difficult people, as well as recognizing what "pushes your buttons" improves how effectively you react.

8

It All Starts with You

Do you have a colleague at work you dread working with? Maybe it's someone who never listens to your opinions, but constantly criticizes them? Perhaps it's someone who is loud and aggressive, and who bullies you into getting their own way? Or perhaps it's that person who's always "pushing your buttons" and pestering you about trivial things? In every workplace there are difficult people like these. You could resign yourself to the situation and blame them for every negative thing that happens. Or you could try to convince them of the error of their ways by arguing your case over and over again.

The truth is though, that neither of these approaches is likely to work. A better approach is to realize that you are not going to change the people around you. The only person you can change is yourself. So it makes sense to work on your own perspective to help reshape your view of difficult people. There are various ways you can do this.

The first way is to accept that difficult people exist. So it's important to learn how to manage your interactions with them more successfully. The second way is to become self-aware. You need to realize that the way you're currently looking at a situation is not the only way to look at it. In fact, there may be a different way of looking at it that will serve you better in the long run. The third way is to manage your emotions and reactions, and learn how to stay calm under pressure. For one thing, feeling stressed all day at work due to constant conflict with others means your own performance will suffer.

So try to rise above it. Maintain an emotional distance when you're dealing with difficult people. Set boundaries and decide when and where you will engage with them. It's better to walk away and think of a logical plan of action rather than getting embroiled in on-the-fly arguments. Finally, you should examine your own temperament and the way you interact with others.

If you find you are too focused on the problems you're facing, try focusing on solutions instead. Instead of thinking constantly about how annoying that difficult person is, try focusing on how you can handle them better. By looking inward in this way, you'll regain control and you'll experience less stress when you interact with difficult people.

9

Becoming Self-Aware

Everyone knows we should pay attention to our physical fitness, but many people don't realize the importance of looking after their emotional fitness too. To build emotional fitness, you need to understand what happens when difficult people "push your buttons" and then be self-aware in the way you respond to them.

You Can't Change Them

There are several ways to increase your self-awareness. The first way is to make time in your day for reflection. By giving yourself the time and space to reflect on what is happening inside you as you interact with others, you'll be better able to identify and manage your own emotions. It will also give you the chance to pause long enough to avoid reacting in a negative way.

When you identify what you are feeling, you can then take the next step of transforming the negative responses into productive and healthy ones. So listen to your mind and body when you're dealing with difficult people. The difficult person's behavior may be toxic, but you can still control your response to it. If you don't stop and reflect, it's likely you'll continue to react in your usual way and end up feeling stressed, angry, or upset when a different response could have made a difficult encounter more effective.

The second way to become more self-aware is to remind yourself that the difficult person's behavior is an example of being "unaware" and set a higher standard for yourself. Difficult people may be genuinely unaware of the negative impact their behavior has on others, or they may delight in causing stress and chaos wherever they go. Either way, you can manage your reaction to their bad behavior and channel your energies into your own "emotional fitness" regime.

The third way of increasing your self-awareness is to name the emotion you're feeling without acting on it. For example, if you feel embarrassed, that doesn't mean you have to apologize or demean yourself. If you feel intimidated or afraid, you don't have to run away or concede.

The final way is to realize that no matter how difficult a person is, you can stay present and in control of yourself when you are emotionally fit. This should lead to more successful interactions with the people around you. It should also help you succeed in the workplace and become more creative, positive, and productive at work.

10

The Self-Aware Response

To deal with difficult people successfully, you first need to learn how to manage yourself. This means being self-aware. When you know what triggers you and how you typically react, you can build skills to make your interactions with others more productive. So next time another person does something to trigger an emotional reaction in you, pay attention. If that feeling is positive and productive – great! But when you feel intimidated, annoyed, frustrated, or angry, others will sense it, you will show it, and you may even internalize it.

The good news is that it's possible to "flip" your response into something more productive. To do this, you have to first identify what you're actually feeling. Consider Julia's situation. She's just been insulted by her boss, Seth, in a meeting. He told her the report she's working on "will be too much for her" and suggested handing it over to another colleague. Julia takes a moment to reflect after the meeting. She knows her boss has pushed her buttons again. She notices that her heart is thumping and she feels humiliated.

However, she also recognizes that she feels this way because her boss is rude and lacks leadership skills. She e-mails him later that day to thank him for his suggestion, and informs him she will complete the report later that week. Julia can't change her boss, but she has preserved her dignity through self-awareness.

So how can you flip your response around using self-awareness? You can follow three steps. First, slow down and take note of how your body is responding to the emotional trigger. It could be that you're breathing too hard, or you may notice your heart is beating a little too fast. Ask yourself, "Why is this person's behavior making me respond this way?" By recognizing the physiological changes taking place, you are demonstrating self-awareness.

The second step is to examine your own feelings without judgment. Admit that you may feel fearful, disrespected, unappreciated or embarrassed. But don't judge yourself for these feelings, just notice them. The final step is the consciously move from reactive, negative feelings to a thoughtful, reasonable response. To do this, you need to nudge the unconscious, reactive, primal reactions into a thoughtful and reasonable part of your mind.

By managing your emotions in this way, you'll be able to transform a negative response into a more positive one.

11

Did I Say That Out Loud?

You can't make other people less difficult. So your challenge every day is to deal more effectively with the difficult people you meet. To do this effectively, you need to manage your emotions when interacting with the people around you. But how do you know when it's time to step in and actively manage your emotions? There are a number of warning responses that act as "red flags" and that you should pay attention to.

The first warning sign is feeling angry or responding in an angry way to a difficult person. You might find yourself saying things like, "who does she think she is?", or "she has no idea what she's asking!" The second warning sign is feeling adamant in your response to a difficult encounter. This kind of response stops you exploring if there is another way of viewing the situation that might ultimately be beneficial to you. So take note if you hear yourself saying something like, "absolutely not, no way!", or "that's easy for him to say."

The third warning sign is finding yourself being shocked by an insult. When that happens, you might hear yourself say, "excuse me, did he just say what I

You Can't Change Them

thought he said?", or "I cannot believe she just said that!" The fourth warning sign is feeling edgy and impatient in relation to someone else's behavior. When you feel like that, you might say, "is he ever going to get that done?", or "what is wrong with him?"

The fifth warning sign is getting annoyed or being irked by someone else's behavior. So watch out if you hear yourself making comments like, "that's ridiculous", or "that will never work." The sixth and final warning sign is fearing the hostile behavior of another person. When you're fearful, you might say, "I'm so afraid of the repercussions of that", or "I dread my next meeting with him."

When you feel like responding in any of these ways, it's important to recognize that you're actually engaged in negative self-talk. Negative self-talk often makes the situation you're dealing with even worse. It usually creates – and prolongs – negative emotions and stress. It's self-defeating and unnecessary. So next time you're involved in a touchy interaction with a difficult person, take a moment before you say anything. Examine your instinctual emotional reactions. And then focus on managing any negative self-talk.

12

The Meditative Approach

When you're dealing with a difficult person, a variety of negative emotions might start running through your brain. You might feel like responding in an angry way. You might feel edgy and impatient. If these kinds of emotional reactions are actually expressed, it can make the difficult person's behavior even worse. Rather than putting negative self-talk into action, it's better to take control of your responses and manage your emotions. To do this successfully, you need to focus on your own self-management skills.

There are a number of self-management techniques you can practice to improve your skills in this area. For example, you can practice a number of calming, meditative techniques. Calming, meditative techniques help you pay attention to your breath and your body, guiding your feelings to a relaxed state. In this state, you feel calmer and better able to manage your emotional response to a difficult person.

The practice of meditation allows you to recover from emotional "hijacks." So when a difficult person triggers a reaction in your brain, such as surprise, anger, or disgust, you can slow down your "primitive" response and avoid reacting too quickly or inappropriately. Meditation also puts you in a frame of mind where you can visualize difficult people in a more positive light, and even empathize with them. This can make your encounters with them easier.

To meditate, you can practice three techniques. The first technique is calming breathing. To practice this technique, you inhale slowly and then exhale twice as long as you inhaled. For example, inhale to the count of three and exhale to the count of six.

The second technique is muscle relaxation. To practice this technique, sit where you are supported,

You Can't Change Them

for example, on a chair or couch. Begin by feeling the support. Then, beginning with your head or your feet, slowly relax each muscle group until you have attended to each part of your body.

The third technique you could try is visualization. To practice this technique, relax and visualize a place that you find comforting or beautiful, or that elicits positive emotions in you. You can also use guided meditation with music and words to visualize relaxing scenes and sensations.

Spending a few minutes in meditation can restore your calm and inner peace. By practicing meditative techniques, you'll be better able to compose yourself and regulate your emotions after a confrontation with a difficult person.

13

The Thinking Approach

There are a number of self-management techniques you can use to manage your emotions when working with difficult people. For example, you could consider exploring thinking techniques. Thinking techniques call on your brain's ability to regulate your instinctive emotions and neutralize them. By doing this, you avoid acting on raw emotions without thinking.

There are three ways you can practice thinking techniques. The first way is to change your self-talk. Self-talk is another name for your inner voice, the voice in your head which says things that you don't necessarily say out loud. Often self-talk happens without you even realizing it. However, what you say in your head can have an enormous impact on how you feel about yourself. Since self-talk can be both positive and negative, it makes sense to try to engage in better, more positive self-talk.

So try "talking back" to your negative self-talk. For example, if you're fuming about something and your self-talk tells you, "I'm going to strike back!", change direction by telling yourself, "even though I'm feeling upset, I trust that I'll deal with this effectively." This may seem simplistic, but it helps to move you into a positive emotional state rather than a negative one.

The second way to practice thinking techniques is by goal intention. Set a goal for yourself in relation to managing yourself when you're around a difficult person. Think about moving yourself in the direction of your goal using intention. Visualize the end result of reaching the goal, and take time during each day to think about that achieved goal.

The third way to practice thinking techniques is by using logic. Use logic to reframe and recalibrate negative emotions. Even if you can't "talk yourself out of it," you can neutralize the emotion. For example, imagine sliding the intensity of an emotion you're feeling down from "intense" to "neutral". Ask yourself if it makes sense to maintain your emotion at a high level and consider the logic of neutralizing it in order to better manage yourself.

Try the different techniques and see which works best for you. You can mix and match them, and choose the ones that are most suited to a particular situation.

And remember, it takes time to build self-management skills. Practice makes perfect. So if it doesn't work the first time, don't give up. These are skills well worth investing in.

14

Identifying Your Own Difficulty Style

Take a moment to look around your office. You may notice that people you work with display a variety of different personality styles, values, and temperaments. Teams with a mix of personalities can be both productive and motivating, but they can also experience clashes and disharmony. Think about it. You probably prefer working with some of your colleagues more than others.

It's important to realize that your preferences stem from your own temperament, personality style, and values, not theirs. Unless you understand the relationship between your own temperament and the way you perceive others, you'll probably waste a lot of time expecting others to change.

It's better to focus on identifying your own personality style and the preferences that affect your feelings about others. When you recognize your own preferences, you can moderate your behavior to work better with other people. One way to do this is to examine four main personality types and discover which category you belong to, and which category the people around you fall into.

The first personality type is called Dominant-Controlling. People who belong in this category can be described as fast-acting, outgoing, bold, and assertive. They like challenges and they can get impatient with people who are slow or indecisive.

The second personality type is known as Analytical-Obsessive. People who exhibit analytical-obsessive behavior are methodical, logical, and detail-oriented. They like perfection, and have trouble making decisions or letting go of anything that isn't perfect.

The third personality type is Expressive-Impulsive. If you fall into this category, you're likely someone who can be described as enthusiastic, people-oriented, optimistic, and social. You may like motivating others, but probably have trouble with details or follow-through.

The final personality type is called Skeptical-Negative. People who fall into this category are more interested in what is bad than what is good. They complain, whine, and at times behave like a victim. They pull people down instead of raising them up. They can also be quite adamant and opinionated in their views.

So which description seems most like you? Which description fits that difficult colleague of yours? When you know which category you fall into, you can take steps to adapt your personality and temperament in different situations. This should help you have more harmonious interactions with difficult people.

You Can't Change Them

15

Avoid Becoming a Difficult Person

Do you realize you're probably considered to be a "difficult person" by at least one other person in your office? The good news is that when you recognize your own personal temperament and style of behavior, you can take steps to adapt your style, so it blends more harmoniously with the styles of the people around you. Let's examine the behavior you can engage in to overcome the negative conduct that's associated with each of the four main personality types.

The first personality type is Dominant-Controlling. If you fall into this category, you may be viewed by others as being dominant, demanding, controlling, or impatient. To avoid this, ask people for their opinions, and make time to explore other viewpoints. When feeling impatient about a decision, ask a person with a more thoughtful or analytical style to help you achieve balance.

The second personality type is Analytical-Obsessive. If you fit in this category, people may view you as being analytical, obsessive, or rigid. To overcome this, discuss the parameters of your projects with others, and find out the level of quality or accuracy that's required. Then you should attempt to meet the standard but not over-exceed it. When you're asked to make a decision, ask a colleague with a different personality type for advice.

The third personality type is Expressive-Impulsive. People in this category are often viewed as being impulsive, excitable, expressive, or self-centered. If you find yourself in this category, soften your tone and voice when speaking with others, and try to listen more than you talk. Ask for opinions and be open to ideas that are different from your own. Write down your plans for carrying out ideas, and try to engage with people who are more organized and detail-oriented than you are.

The final personality type is Skeptical-Negative. If you belong in this category, people may view you as being skeptical, negative, pessimistic, cynical, or doubtful. To prevent this, try to avoid getting drawn into negative conversations. Instead, simply listen and acknowledge what you've heard. Ask how the situation could be improved or changed, and try to steer the discussion in a more positive direction.

The goal of adapting your behavior to different situations is not to change who you are. Instead, it's to help you recognize your own role in difficult interactions, which should help you work better with people who have different styles.

Part III

Working Together

Difficult people exist – and no workplace is without them. The good news is that as well as managing your own emotions and getting personally fit, there are interpersonal strategies you can use to deal with difficult people.

16

Keeping Things Interpersonal

When it comes to dealing with difficult people, it makes sense to work on improving your own emotional fitness. When you're emotionally fit, you can manage your emotions and reactions better. And you can use self-management techniques to reshape your view of difficult people.

However, as well as personal skills such as these, there are a number of interpersonal strategies you should master in order to engage successfully with difficult people, and keep them on track.

The first strategy is to focus on your goals. To put this strategy into action, you need to put your work goals at the top of your agenda – and keep them there.

This strategy involves asking everyone to focus on the main goal to be accomplished. Then ask all parties to agree on the best way of achieving that goal. If anyone's behavior becomes "difficult" at a later stage, you can then redirect that person toward the goal – and the behaviors everyone agreed were necessary to achieve it.

The second strategy is to give feedback directly to the difficult person. This means attempting to change the person's challenging behavior, so it's more suited to the situation you find yourself in.

As long as the difficult person isn't being bullying or abusive, this approach gives you the opportunity to validate the person by accepting his or her personality style for what it is; while at the same time asking for a different approach and more moderate behavior.

The third strategy is to manage conflict. Not all dealings with difficult people result in a full-blown conflict. But if, in the process of working together, you and another person clash on a subject or issue and cannot resolve the situation, you'll need to actively manage the conflict.

As you implement this strategy, you'll need to be sensitive to the kinds of words that work and don't work in relation to that person's personality type. For example, being overly analytical probably won't help resolve the situation if the person you're dealing with has a more expressive or dominant personality.

Of course, there are other interpersonal strategies you can use to cope with difficult people when all else fails, or when your common sense guides you to do so.

For example, you could escalate the issue to your manager, discuss the difficulty with another person you trust, or even simply walk away from the person.

Whatever strategy you decide to use, having a variety of personal skills and interpersonal strategies at your disposal gives you the best chance of dealing successfully with difficult people.

17

Developing Ground Rules

Typically, whatever you're working on has a goal or a desired outcome. Whether you're working independently or as part of a team, "difficult" people can derail your plans and interfere with your goals.

One of the best ways to redirect the behavior of difficult people towards your goal is to establish ground rules at the outset of a project. While it's possible to create ad-hoc ground rules when difficult behavior arises, it's much easier if ground rules have been discussed and agreed on from the start.

Ground rules express the kind of behavior that's required to achieve a goal. These are rules that everyone must try to honor, for the good of the project.

Ground rules will vary according to the situation, but some rules are fairly common. Rules that relate to keeping order might include "speak one at a time and listen to others" or "everyone participates and no person should dominate."

Rules related to keeping things running on time might be "adhere to the agenda and create a 'parking lot' for extraneous issues," "stay focused on the issues and avoid personal comments," or "be concise and to the point."

And there may be rules for actions after the meeting, such as "ask questions when you don't understand or need further clarification" or "share information with others."

Whatever ground rules you choose, it's not difficult to imagine that some of them would be difficult for "difficult" people to accept. For example, Dominant-Controlling personality types find it difficult to listen to others and want to dominate every discussion.

So people of this personality type are likely to resist ground rules where they're asked to speak one at a time and listen to others, let others participate equally, or share information with team members.

Analytical-Obsessive personality types are detail-oriented perfectionists, who have trouble making decisions and letting go of anything that isn't perfect.

Expressive-Impulsive people can be disorganized, and have trouble with details or follow-through. They are likely to resist ground rules where they're asked to stick to an agenda or ask questions if they don't understand something.

Finally, Skeptical-Negative individuals are more interested in what is bad than what is good. They complain a lot and can be quite opinionated in their views.

Clearly, ground rules are a useful way of redirecting the behavior of difficult people towards your goal. You can expect resistance and "push back" from certain people. Nevertheless, your ground rules should still be enforced.

18

Focusing on Goals

Establishing ground rules at the start of a project can help you redirect the behavior of difficult people towards your goals and desired outcomes.

However, creating ground rules is one thing — enforcing them is another. Different personality types can respond negatively to ground rules, making them difficult to enforce. Luckily, there are strategies you can use to make ground rules work – even when you're dealing with difficult personalities.

The first strategy is to be diplomatic at all times. So when a difficult person breaks a ground rule, never make demands or inflammatory remarks. Don't ignore the person or make the person feel unaccepted. Instead, try asking some questions. For example, if an overly expressive person is being long-winded and rambling off the point, you could say something like, "I hear you. How does that relate to our goal today?" or "Could you summarize that?"

Or if the person introduces a new issue, say, "That seems to be new information. Can you say more about that?"

Similarly, if a controlling person is dominating a discussion, try saying, "We've agreed that everyone should have the chance to participate. Can we share some other thoughts?"

In this way, you should be able to rein in the difficult person's behavior, while avoiding any unnecessary conflict.

The second strategy involves refocusing people's attention on your goal when necessary. So, for example, if a goal requires meeting a deadline and a person's analysis or expressiveness is slowing things down, you could say something like, "In the interest of getting this done on time, can you move forward?"

You could also ask the person to limit further analysis. Alternatively, you could summarize a few key points or action items and ask the person to focus on those items only. Again, this should help you direct the person's difficult behavior towards your goal.

The final strategy involves constantly emphasizing the goal and what it takes to meet it in team meetings and discussions. So if any person's behavior is not directed toward goal-fulfilling work, try to redirect the behavior accordingly. This strategy can be particularly useful when dealing with analytical people, who tend to get distracted by details, and expressive people, who may get sidetracked. And when difficult people respond to your requests or demonstrate a behavior change, be sure to reinforce the behavior. For example, say, "That was helpful" or "Thank you for listening."

By using these strategies, you'll be able to face the challenges of working with difficult people. And you'll be in a better position to achieve your goals.

19

The Right Time to Give Feedback

Feedback is a highly valuable skill that can benefit all interpersonal communications – so if you can give and receive feedback when working with difficult people, you're mastering a complex skill. The art of giving effective feedback can be learned and perfected. So it makes sense to invest time in mastering this skill. It's important to choose the appropriate time to give feedback to a difficult person. So when is the best time to do this? There are several strategies you can use to ensure you're providing feedback at the right time.

The first strategy is to make sure you can identify specific behaviors and consequences that can be improved if the person changes or modifies his or her behavior. It's not enough to simply tell people they annoy you or they intimidate you — you need to be more specific. So for example, tell the person that by talking so much in a meeting, that person's voice was the only one heard and you weren't able to get to the main point. Or explain that by over-analyzing a problem, the person got lost in the details and missed an important deadline.

The second strategy is to be prepared to give constructive feedback. To be constructive, feedback should focus on solutions, not problems. For example, if you notice a person is taking too long to complete a task, ask the person if there's a better approach to take — and then nudge the person in the right direction by suggesting the correct approach. Avoid being overly negative and make sure you don't scold the person for their behavior. Try to make the feedback session a positive process and experience.

The final strategy is to only provide feedback when you and the difficult person are in an appropriate venue. Ideally, the venue should be a meeting room or private office — feedback should never be provided in a public place. There are times when feedback should not be delivered — such as when the timing isn't right. So avoid giving feedback if the person is distracted with an urgent task or rushing off to a meeting.

Feedback is also best avoided if there is too much emotion involved, such as when you or the difficult person are angry or upset. So wait until everyone has calmed down before you engage in feedback.

Remember, the point of giving feedback is to improve the difficult person's behavior. You'll get the best out of the most difficult people if your feedback is positive and focused on improvement – and if it's delivered at the right time.

20

Delivering Feedback

If you work with a difficult person whose behavior is threatening to derail your project, you need to give them feedback – and fast. Giving feedback can be a delicate process. Luckily, there are strategies you can use to deliver feedback in the most effective way.

The first strategy is to deliver the feedback face-to-face whenever you can. If that's not possible, use the telephone. Ideally, feedback should be delivered by talking "live" to the person. So don't use e-mail or leave a voice message.

The second strategy is to emphasize the business reason for providing the feedback. For example, the difficult person might need to adjust their behavior in order to meet a project goal, uphold the company mission, or to meet a specific performance need.

The next strategy is to focus on the difficult behavior and any associated issues – but not on the person. So instead of saying something personal like, "You're too demanding," it's more effective to say,

"When you use language that sounds demanding, I feel like I don't have a say and it slows down our progress."

A fourth strategy is to be specific about the exact behavior you're addressing. Make sure you're prepared with examples. So instead of just saying, "You intimidate everyone in meetings," say something like: "In yesterday's meeting, you dealt with all the issues in a very assertive way. However I think we need to look at getting the rest of the team involved in the decision making."

The fifth strategy is to be responsible for the feedback you deliver. So avoid speaking for other people. Don't say, "Other people feel the same way" or "Even the boss thinks you're too indecisive." Own the feedback you're delivering and be prepared to stand over it.

The sixth strategy is to ask the difficult person to change or modify the difficult behavior you're commenting on. For example, you could ask a person who dominates meetings, "Would you be willing to listen to other views and perspectives?"

The final strategy is to check in and ask the difficult person what he or she thinks about your request or suggestion. You can suggest a follow-up meeting or provide support. But ultimately it's up to the difficult person to make the change you've suggested.

In the end, you may not get the change you'd like immediately, but you'll have addressed the person in a constructive manner. Hopefully, whether the change happens in the short or long term, the person

will remember your feedback and be grateful for
receiving it.

21

Manage Conflict

If you're working with a difficult person, chances
are you have differences. Some of these you might be
able to live with. But others may lead to conflict.
Conflicts typically arise when there is a clash of
styles, perspectives, values, or approaches to
problems between two people. When you find yourself
in conflict with another person, don't lose heart or give
up! It's possible to manage the situation and develop
a more mutually satisfying work relationship.

There are five steps in the process for managing
conflict with another person.

The first step is to agree that there is some conflict
or clash between you. For example, perhaps one
person wants to make a decision while the other
wants to collect more data; one wants to engage
outside resources and the other wants to control the
work in-house; one wants to generate ideas with
coworkers while the other wants to dictate a solution.

The second step is to consider what you know about
the person's style as well as your own style. Armed
with that information, you can figure out how to best
approach the person in a conflict-management
situation. For example, if you recognize the person
you're dealing with is somewhat controlling and

impulsive, a simple gesture like allowing that person to speak first or acknowledging his or her ideas can be helpful.

The third step is to express the problem using words that will facilitate the conversation, rather than intimidating or "shutting down" the other person. So discuss the situation in a respectful manner. Don't lose your temper or get angry. Avoid blaming the other person for the conflict and focus instead on finding common ground and possible solutions.

The fourth step is to ensure both you and the other person get to speak. Remind yourself that your colleague may not be sensitive to the words that "push your buttons" and trigger your emotions, so take a deep breath and be patient if that happens. Be sure to acknowledge the other person's point of view. And keep the discussion focused on how to work together and accomplish your goals.

The final step is to seek a resolution you can both live with, and create some short-term goals so you both can "win." For example, you could both agree to limit the features of a prototype the team is working on. This could result in lower production costs for the next three months – which benefits you; and less pressure on internal resources – which benefits the other person.

When you work with a difficult person to resolve a conflict, it brings you together and often leads to an improved working relationship.

Part IV

Aggressive People

Have you ever encountered someone who broke into a sudden rant? Maybe they said something like "I have never heard anything so ridiculous in my life! You're kidding me right? Why am I the only one with the intelligence to see a problem here?"

This behavior is aggressive – hostile-aggressive, to be precise – and it's one of the most difficult behaviors you'll face.

22

Types of Aggressive People

You may have also encountered the more subtle passive-aggressive behavior. Whether subtle or overt, you have to be prepared to deal with these expressions of aggression in the workplace.

Hostile-aggressive as well as passive-aggressive behaviors are learned, and the basis of each is anger. However, each type also has its own traits.

Hostile-aggressive

Hostile-aggressive behavior is relatively easy to spot. Individuals who behave in this manner are angry. They will often yell and use personal, verbal attacks to get what they want. They are difficult to work with because their personal attacks can raise your own anger and stress levels. It's hard to stay calm and focused when you're treated with disrespect.

Passive-aggressive

Passive-aggressive behavior is more subtle than hostile-aggressive behavior. Passive-aggressive individuals are experts at manipulation and go to great lengths to hide their true intentions. They don't show anger. Passive-aggressive behavior is hard to deal with because you never know what's really going on. You can't trust the intentions of a passive-aggressive person.

Working with Difficult People

23

Benefits of Dealing with Aggression

Does this situation sound familiar to you? Jill and Franco are colleagues. Recently, Franco angrily accused Jill of not pulling her weight. To get Franco off her back, Jill agrees to review a stack of case files that aren't really her responsibility. Jill feels as though she's been bullied into accepting the extra work and her stress level is high.

In this situation, Franco's use of anger to get his way is typical hostile-aggressive behavior. Hostile-aggressives use their bad behavior, such as reacting angrily and being accusatory, to get what they want or to have things their own way.

You will likely face hostile-aggressive behavior at work. You may think ignoring it is a viable option, but this is unrealistic. Also, dealing with hostile-aggressive behavior provides benefits you'll want to take advantage of:

- increased productivity
- improved self-esteem, and
- a regained sense of control

Increased productivity

Dealing effectively with hostile-aggressive people helps you reduce the stress caused by their bad behavior. And a less stressful work environment facilitates improved health and increased workplace productivity.

Improved self-esteem

Improved self-esteem is another possible benefit. Suppose you interpret a hostile-aggressive person's behavior as a personal attack – this can be damaging to your self-esteem. Learning to effectively handle hostile-aggressive behavior will reduce its damaging effects, plus you'll feel a sense of accomplishment.

Regained sense of control

It can be hard to deal with hostile-aggressive behavior calmly. You may find yourself losing control or feeling like you've lost control. Knowing how to deal with hostile-aggressive behavior can help you regain your sense of control. This will allow you to avoid being drawn into the negative behavior, so you're part of the solution and not part of the problem.

24

Hostile-aggressive behavior

Hostile-aggressive individuals are bullies and controllers. Their general method of operation is to look strong by making others look weak. It's not unusual for them to yell during exchanges with others, and they tend to be offensive, belligerent, and bad listeners. And they typically have a resentful attitude.

People with hostile-aggressive personalities are sometimes classified as two types: the verbal assailant and the hothead.

Verbal assailant

Verbal assailants tend to attack with words. They come across as openly abusive and tend to be abrupt, intimidating, and overwhelming. They attack at the personal level and generally pick an aspect of an individual's behavior or personality to fuel the attack.

Hothead

Hotheads are prone to sudden outbursts of anger and rage, even when everything seems to be going well. A hothead's anger tends to be triggered when the individual perceives a physical or psychological threat. The hothead's anger is likely to be followed by fear and suspicion.

C onsider this example of typical hostile-aggressive behavior you might witness when dealing with a verbal assailant. Caroline is a soft-spoken, competent, and knowledgeable woman. She's in a team meeting when she makes a suggestion to build on one of her colleague's ideas. The idea is Candice's, and she has a hostile-aggressive personality.

Follow along to find out how Candice reacts to Caroline's suggestion.

Caroline: What if we add a "worst-case" scenario plan? That way the client will know we're prepared for all possible outcomes.
Caroline says, genuinely.

Candice: What was that Caroline? I couldn't hear you. If you want to be taken seriously, at least have the conviction to express yourself with confidence instead of in a mousy, noncommittal way!
Candice says, angrily.

In this example, Candice felt threatened by Caroline's contribution. True to verbal assailant form, Candice responded with a verbal attack on Caroline. She perceives Caroline's soft-spoken nature as a weakness and angrily attacked Caroline based on this personal characteristic

25

Handling Hostile-Aggressives

Understanding why a person acts in a hostile-aggressive manner can help you effectively handle this behavior.

Where does hostile-aggressive behavior come from? It's a learned behavior. Hostile-aggressive behavior is a form of control. Individuals who interact in a hostile-aggressive way have learned that by being difficult, they get what they want.

Even though they come across as strong and confident, often the reality is that they're frightened and insecure. Acting with hostility and aggression is how these individuals achieve a feeling of safety, power, and control.

Have you ever been left feeling bullied or taken advantage of after a dealing with a coworker? If so, you may have been on the receiving end of hostile-aggressive behavior. You may also have been left feeling vulnerable, provoked, angry, frustrated, powerless, or confused.

There's a seven-step process that can help you handle hostile-aggressive behavior. The process involves distancing yourself, assessing the situation, thinking about how you'll respond, assuring the other party you're listening, discussing the problem further, offering your point of view, and monitoring your success.

The first step in handling hostile-aggressive behavior is to distance yourself from the situation emotionally, and physically if necessary.

Distance yourself by depersonalizing the situation. Remember that the person is probably reacting to an issue or a culmination of issues that actually have nothing to do with you, so it's best that you don't take it personally. It also helps to stay neutral and remain calm.

Taking it personally and failing to stay calm increases the likelihood that you'll react angrily, which will only escalate the situation. It's important

Aggressive People

that, even though the attack is personal and inappropriate, you don't respond in kind.

The second step is assessing the situation. Actively listen while the hostile-aggressive person says all they have to say.

Don't interrupt and don't respond until you have both calmed down. Interjecting while either of you is upset can make things worse. Also, if you're reacting, you're not listening. You may misunderstand and prolong the incident.

The third step is thinking about how you'll respond. This helps ensure you respond in the most effective way. When the person is done venting and you can respond, you will move on to step four – assuring the other party you're listening.

Think about how you'll respond

Consider what you've learned from actively listening and think carefully about how you'll respond to effectively address the situation. Remember to hold your commentary until the hostile-aggressive person has finished.

Assure the other party you're listening

Once the person has finished venting, give assurance that you're listening by summarizing what you've understood the person to say.

Now that you have achieved understanding, politely offer to discuss the problem further; this is step five. Such a discussion can improve understanding of the situation, allowing for a speedier and more complete resolution. It can also give you more insight on how to handle the hostile-aggressive person in the future.

In step six, offering your point of view, you can explain how you feel. You should also give the other person an opportunity to reflect, gather thoughts, and return to the discussion if necessary.

The final step, step seven, is to monitor your success. Following a hostile-aggressive encounter, you should take the time to evaluate how well your approach worked. Learn from your successes as well as your mistakes and use this information in future dealings with hostile-aggressive coworkers.

D anica and Jasper are technical writers. They often discuss particular challenges they're facing. Today, Danica is having trouble describing something and has asked Jasper for his input. The discussion is progressing nicely when Jasper comments that he can't believe Danica is having such trouble. Danica immediately and angrily retorts "Well, obviously you can't do any better or you'd be helping instead of criticizing. I don't know why I even bothered to ask!"

Jasper realizes he's made Danica angry and he needs to deal with the situation. He follows several steps:

- he distances himself from the situation by reminding himself that he shouldn't take Danica's outburst personally

- with his composure intact, he listens carefully to what Danica is saying, and
- he thinks about how he'll respond when she's finished
- Now that Danica has finished, follow along as Jasper attempts to deal with her hostile-aggressive outburst.

Jasper: Danica, I understand what I said was disrespectful. And I understand why you're upset.
Jasper says, sincerely.

Danica: Well I should hope so!
Danica says, excitedly.

Jasper: I'm willing to explore this situation with you if you'd like. I don't want there to be any bad blood between us.
Jasper says, sincerely.

Danica: No, thanks. I don't see the point of discussing it any further. You understand why I was upset and I appreciate you acknowledging you were wrong.
Danica says, flatly.

Jasper: That's fair, but I would like to point out that I never meant to come across as disrespectful. I was thinking that perhaps you were off your game, under the weather, or stressed, because you usually excel at describing these complex ideas. Can you see that?

Jasper says, kindly.

Danica: Really? Hmm...I guess I can accept that that's where you were going with your comment.
Danica sounds interested.

Jasper: I can see how you could take it wrong. I didn't do a good job of expressing myself. It's important to talk these things through – I don't want a misunderstanding to diminish our work relationship.
Jasper says, kindly.

After his confrontation with Danica, Jasper reflects on the incident. He knew Danica could behave in a hostile-aggressive manner, but had never been on the receiving end before. Now that he has, he knows that a humble approach can help get Danica past her anger and move the situation toward resolution.

26

Passive-Aggressive Behavior

Have you ever had a coworker who seemed pleasant and competent but then let you down? Maybe he agreed to provide data for a project but failed to produce it? Or maybe she agreed to contribute to a project, but didn't?

These are examples of typical passive-aggressive behavior. If you've experienced something like this, maybe you were concerned that you were overreacting or misinterpreting the situation.

Feeling angry is normal when you're on the receiving end of passive-aggressive behavior because anger and fear are the driving emotions behind the behavior. Passive-aggressive behavior is far more subtle than hostile-aggressive behavior and just as hard, if not harder, to handle.

People with passive-aggressive personalities typically come across as quiet and shy. Additionally, you'll notice they're always nice, never defend themselves, and don't assert themselves.

You can also recognize passive-aggressive people by other common behaviors:

- talking about others, in a harmful way, behind their backs
- playing dumb to either frustrate others or gain some type of advantage
- not taking responsibility for their actions, and
- rarely saying what they really mean

Passive-aggressive personality types want to be understood as nice, agreeable, and helpful, and they work very hard to project this image.

The key to the behavior of passive-aggressive people is their inability to be assertive. This means they say "yes" when they want to say "no." They commit to work or tasks they don't want to do.

Passive-aggressive people are full of anger and fear. Unable to say "no," they end up doing things they don't want to and feel resentful about it. They sabotage work efforts and avoid fulfilling commitments they've made, all while maintaining a facade of pleasantness. Experience has taught them that this is how to deal with their unexpressed fear and anger. Passive-aggressive behavior may manifest as missed deadlines, broken promises, poorly done work, the silent treatment, and the use of excuses to justify actions.

Based on their typical behavior, passive-aggressive individuals generally fall into one of three categories: the knowledge warden, the unresponsive aggressor, and the waffler.

Knowledge warden

Passive-aggressive types who refuse to part with information in their control are known as knowledge wardens.

A knowledge warden will make excuses that you can't reasonably counter without looking insensitive or unreasonable, and then they'll withhold the information you need to do your job.

Unresponsive aggressor

The unresponsive aggressor appears uninterested in communicating and may fail to respond to questions.

Unresponsive aggressors may hesitate when asked a question. As they hesitate, you may move on or make a decision without them. This is a stall tactic that is intended to frustrate or impede efficient, productive work.

Waffler

Another passive-aggressive type, the waffler, hates to make decisions, always wants to be on the winning side, and desperately wants the approval of others. The waffler will do whatever it takes to avoid making a commitment. This is a clever way to impede work or exert control over a situation.

C onsider this example. During a team meeting, Ava agrees to supply a return on investment (ROI) projection for a project. The ROI results are a major decision-making factor and therefore it's vital that the team have them before moving ahead with the project. Ava secretly resents having been asked to do the ROI.

Follow along to find out how Ava reacts as she depicts each of the three passive-aggressive types, and the impact her reaction might have on the project and project leader, Jack.

<u>**Knowledge warden:**</u> Jack's having a hard time getting the ROI information from Ava. He's tried contacting her via e-mail and phone, but his requests for updates have been ignored. Every time the team has a meeting, Ava pleasantly offers some excuse and insists she's just about done. Meanwhile, the project has stalled. Jack may have to reassign the task.

Working with Difficult People 79

Unresponsive aggressor: Jack and Ava are meeting to discuss the ROI results. Jack finds getting the information difficult. He's not sure if Ava's silence and hesitation are a sign that the ROI is bad, that there's something wrong with her, or that she's angry with him for some reason. Whatever it is, it's frustrating and a waste of time. He can't spend all day trying to figure out what's wrong – he just needs to know the ROI results.

Waffler: Jack asks questions, but Ava never gives him a straight answer. Ava's the one with the experience, but she insists that Jack decide how to interpret the results. Jack wasn't intending to do any work on this. He expected a completed ROI that the team could use to make a decision. This is slowing down the team's progress.

These examples demonstrate that while each type of passive-aggressive behavior is different in technique, the result is the same. Situations get complicated and passive-aggressive people are able to assert some control over the situation. This helps them act on their resentment while still maintaining a pleasant and helpful persona.

27

Handling Passive-Aggressives

Handling passive-aggressive behavior is tricky. In fact, the best way to handle it is to not react at all. Passive-aggressive individuals are trying to get a reaction out of you. If they can upset you, all the better. This is the only way they know how to interact.

If you don't react, the passive-aggressive behavior will typically stop – for the time being, anyway. When you don't react as expected, the passive-aggressive individual won't know what to do.

Passive-aggressive individuals are usually unaware of their behavior, which is why you really can't do anything to change it. However, assertiveness training has been shown to be an effective way of encouraging passive-aggressive people to learn better ways of interacting with others.

Learning how to say "no" – and knowing that it's OK to do so – gives the passive-aggressive person an alternative to always saying "yes" and then being angry about it.

You can use three steps to help you handle passive-aggressive behavior in the workplace. Begin by starting documentation, then confront the individual about specific incidents, and, finally, provide positive reinforcement.

The first step in the process is to start documentation. Document when and what you asked the passive-aggressive individual to do. This way, if things go wrong because of a passive-aggressive person's failure to do the job, you can prove that it wasn't your fault.

Perhaps you have to work with someone you know is passive aggressive. Be proactive and start documentation. For example, send an e-mail clearly outlining what you've asked for and expect.

The second step in handling passive-aggressive behavior is to confront the individual about specific incidents. Just state what happened and its impact.

For instance, say something like "You agreed you'd deliver the completed paperwork by the end of the day Monday, and you didn't. This means I can't live up to my commitment."

Don't get personal and attack the person's character or personality. Keep your focus on the incident itself.

Greg and Anita are coworkers. Anita's supposed to help Greg by photocopying a proposal he's just finished. He's leery about working with Anita because she's let him down in the past. As Greg suspected, Anita didn't photocopy the proposal. Follow along as Greg speaks to Anita about the incident.

Greg: Anita, do you have a moment? I'd like to talk to you privately.
Greg says, seriously.

Anita: Sure Greg, anything for you.
Anita says, pleasantly.

Greg: Anita, I asked you to have the proposal ready at a specific time. I was counting on you and you let me down. I had to stay late to do the work myself.
Greg says, seriously.

Anita: I'm sorry Greg, I couldn't get to the photocopier because Sally in finance was printing off reports. Honestly, the situation was beyond my control.
Anita says, apologetically.

In this brief conversation, Greg did a great job of sticking to the facts and not making the incident personal. Anita was pleasant but still making excuses, a common passive-aggressive tactic. Confronting the individual offers a chance for passive-aggressive people to see you're on to their tactics, hopefully forcing them to find a more appropriate way to interact.

Step three in handling passive-aggressive behavior is to provide positive reinforcement. Positive reinforcement is given only when passive-aggressive individuals do what was asked and expected of them.

When this happens, it's important that you acknowledge the effort. Show appreciation for the work they've done by telling them how helpful they were, and the positive impact it had.

Suppose that in the previous example, Anita did get the proposal ready on time. Greg could provide positive reinforcement by saying something like "I just wanted to let you know I got that proposal submitted on time. You did an excellent job compiling and copying the proposal. I really appreciate the work you put in to make that happen. Thank you."

Greg's positive reinforcement might be just what it takes to build a positive, productive relationship with Anita. This may help Anita see that she doesn't have to be passive-aggressive.

Everyone likes to be acknowledged and appreciated for the work they do. For passive-aggressive individuals, it's a chance to see that contributing can bring positive rewards, and it shows them a different way to interact. The payoff for you is that you build a relationship where you can rely on this individual to do what you ask, allowing you to do your own job more efficiently and productively.

However, if you've tried these steps and been unsuccessful in getting the passive-aggressive person's cooperation, you have a few more options you can try.

The options are to use leverage, get support from your coworkers, and get help from your supervisor.

Use leverage

If you have leverage, use it. Here, your documentation will be useful. Reminding the passive-aggressive individual of the commitment she made can prompt her to do the work. You can also try reminding her that one day, she may need your help.

Get support from your coworkers

Your coworkers are likely to have knowledge that can help you deal with the passive-aggressive individual, so get support from them. There's also power in numbers. If you and your coworkers unite, you may be able to convince your supervisor that the negative impact of the passive-aggressive individual's behavior is significant and needs to be dealt with.

Get help from your supervisor

You can also get help from your supervisor. Express how the individual's behavior is negatively impacting your productivity, and ask for advice on how to handle the situation. If you choose to approach your supervisor, make sure you're prepared with facts and specific examples. Again, your documentation will prove useful.

28

Working with Hostile-Aggressives

You'll likely face hostile-aggressive behavior at work. Being prepared for it can help you handle the situation more effectively and minimize the impact of the negative behavior. You'll recognize hostile-aggressive individuals by their difficult behavior, which is likely to be laced with hostility, anger, and resentment. Their exchanges often involve yelling and offensive and belligerent behavior.

Effectively handling hostile-aggressive people so you can get back to work takes finesse. A seven-step process can help.

The seven steps are to distance yourself from the situation emotionally, assess the situation, think about how you'll respond, assure the other party you're listening, discuss the problem further, offer your point of view, and monitor your success.

C onsider this example. A home renovation company has spent countless hours trying to satisfy a customer who can't be satisfied. George, the operations manager, is not happy. He thinks the company should cut its losses and let the customer go. James, the customer care manager, wants to make things right and turn this experience into a good one for the customer.

George storms into James's office, shaking his fist and yelling. Follow along to find out what George had to say.

George: "What are you thinking? I don't think you are thinking! The customer is not always right, James!"

George: "Mrs. Hutchins is unreasonable and can't be pleased. Our work is impeccable. I can't justify the expense, and while we cater to her, my guys are falling behind schedule with other projects."

George: "The problem is she keeps changing her mind. How long are we going to pay for her indecisiveness? Come on James – get real and dump Mrs. Hutchins."

James is taken aback by George's outburst. His anger is overwhelming, but James remembers the first rule of dealing with hostile-aggressive behavior and emotionally distances himself from the situation. He knows this isn't personal and that George is just frustrated with the situation.

Instead of interrupting, James allows George to speak his mind. Meanwhile, he listens carefully to make sure he picks up on the relevant information. This will help him respond more appropriately when George is finished. James thinks acknowledging George's concerns about the loss and the impact on other projects will be a good way to respond.

Now that George is done venting and has calmed down, James feels he can begin a discussion by recapping George's valid points, leaving his emotions out of it. Follow along as James and George explore the situation and look for mutual ground.

James: George, I understand that we're losing money on this project. And the impact on other projects is something we will have to address immediately. Would you like to discuss how we'll handle this now?
James says, concerned.

George: Well, there's no time like the present. And since we've got our cards on the table, let's get this over with.

George says, abruptly.

James: I'm concerned as well. And I agree that Mrs. Hutchins is difficult to work with. She's taking advantage of our commitment to customer satisfaction by changing her mind about what she wants.
James says, calmly.

George: I'm glad to hear it; I was beginning to wonder if you'd lost your senses.
George says, relieved.

James: I have a proposal. I'll contact Mrs. Hutchins and explain our predicament. We'll finish the work upholding our exemplary standards, but we won't make any further design, material, or aesthetic changes unless she wants to pay. Does that sound fair?
James says, calmly.

George: I have one concern. I can't keep dedicating resources to her job at the expense of other customers. If she's willing to pay for additional changes, we'll do them, but she'll have to wait.
George sounds concerned.

James: I agree. That sounds fair. I'll do my best to make sure she feels the same.
James says, enthusiastically.

At this point, James offers to discuss the matter further if George thinks of any other concerns after he leaves James's office. James also invites George to share anything he thinks will help resolve the issue with Mrs. Hutchins. At the end of the day, James makes notes about this incident. He hopes that by noting what worked and what didn't he will learn how to effectively work with George.

James used the seven-step process to work with George. Distancing himself emotionally allowed him to remain calm. Listening and not interrupting helped James focus on what George was saying and gave him time to think about how he'd respond. Remaining polite and positive as he discussed the issue helped James build rapport and move toward resolution of the issue. While, offering his input helped further express his interest in George's concern. Finally, monitoring his success will help James learn from the experience.

Part V

Negative People

Every workplace has someone whose negative behavior affects the harmony and efficiency of the workplace. These people whine that others in the office aren't supporting their efforts, and worst of all, they often blame coworkers for their own mistakes.

29

Types of Negative People

When you have to work with difficult people, their behavior makes it hard to relate productively to them. These behaviors can impact coworkers harmfully and derail productivity.

Negative people are the type who try to relate to others in ways that grate on the nerves and strip away the tolerance of coworkers.

Sadly, many people either just give up trying to create a positive change and settle for ignoring their difficult coworker, or they adopt negative behavior themselves.

Dealing with people is a part of life. When relationships are positive, you can reap all sorts of emotional and tangible rewards. But when you run up against negative people, it can have the opposite effect.

Why do people behave negatively at work? Often it's because negative behavior has benefited them in the past. But there are many other motivating factors:

- attempting to satisfy personal needs or agendas
- seeking attention or validation
- dealing with feelings of fear or inadequacy
- relieving stress
- displacing anger, and
- rationalizing that their own needs are more important than teamwork

Whatever their motivation for behaving negatively, it's important to approach these difficult people proactively. Rewarding aspects of dealing with these people can be the challenge of finding a solution to their issues and establishing positive, productive work relationships.

Negative people are often described by their character types. But the terms whiner, blamer, and complainer aren't judgments about people. Rather, those descriptions relay the reactive behavior that some difficult people fall into when under stress. When you know how to deal with these types of people, you'll be able to help them move from emotional reaction to effective action.

30

Benefits Dealing with Negativity

Many people spend more than half their waking lives at work. When you're at work, your efforts are rewarded, you form friendships and alliances, and often, it's where your core identity is formed. And most people treasure their ability to communicate, socialize, and relate to coworkers in an effective and constructive manner.

Human interaction is part of the social fabric of the workplace. So it's not surprising many issues that arise in the work environment are "people" problems.

Every workplace has a unique blend of people, most of whom are committed to doing the work necessary to develop positive work relationships.

But coworkers have different temperaments, reactive styles, and methods for interacting with others. When you work with other people, sooner or later, you're going to be confronted with negative behavior.

It's important to remember that everyone – even you – can be negative from time to time. But when negative behaviors begin to cause harm to others or derail productivity, it's time to take action.

Negativity can have a detrimental effect on individuals, teams, and organizations.

- One of the consequences of negativity is reduced productivity. When negative behaviors are accepted, they can permeate the workplace and become the norm. Workers in a negative environment spend more time looking for problems than striving to meet their goals.
- Negativity can seriously damage work relationships. Coworkers on the receiving end of negative behaviors can become withdrawn, resentful, or even hostile toward the perpetrator. This can directly affect the cohesion of departments, teams, and workgroups.
- People who manifest negative behavior can affect morale in the workplace. Negativity can be contagious. These perennial "wet blankets" dampen the enthusiasm of coworkers by casting a negative light over their efforts and enthusiasm.

Working with Difficult People   95

You'll gain clear benefits when you can recognize and effectively deal with negative behavior in the workplace:

- you'll increase productivity
- you'll protect your positive outlook, and
- you'll prevent negative behavior from escalating

You'll increase productivity

Difficult people decrease productivity because their negative behavior affects work relationships and team cohesion. Coworkers often react to difficult people by using avoidance. This is particularly problematic when those people are experts in their field or have skills or training necessary to reach team objectives. By learning how to deal with negative people, you can effectively use them as a resource and increase your own productivity.

You'll protect your positive outlook

People who demonstrate negative behavior can emotionally drain coworkers because they cause frustration and stress. Recognizing and dealing effectively with negative behavior can protect your positive outlook and prevent the danger of reacting angrily, obsessing about the situation, or becoming apathetic about your work.

You'll prevent the behavior from escalating

Negative behavior is communication in the form of manipulation. If you don't recognize and deal with the behavior, you subtly signal that it's OK to behave that way. This can escalate problems by encouraging negative people to push the limits of acceptable behavior.

Difficult people often have specific behavioral traits that make them identifiable and, in some ways, predictable. By recognizing and categorizing negative behavior, you can take steps to deal with it.

Three very common behavior types express negativity in the workplace:

- whiners
- complainers, and
- blamers

Managing negativity

Rosalie is dealing with three negative behavior types in her workplace. James is a whiner, Chantal is a complainer, and Vijay is a blamer. But there's hope for Rosalie if she follows three steps for dealing with negative behavior. Step one is listen to the person who is being negative, step two is to demonstrate an understanding of their message, and step three is to try to resolve the issue. This strategy will help Rosalie increase her productivity, protect her positive outlook, and prevent her coworkers' negative behavior from escalating any further.

31

Recognizing Whiners

Differentiating between whiners, complainers and blamers comes down to the focus of their behaviors. Whiners are most often focused on themselves and their perceived burdens – the "poor me" syndrome.

Complainers usually focus their negativity outwardly on specific people or issues, and they aren't content until they feel the perceived problem is resolved.

Reflect

Negative people are sometimes described as "whining and complaining," but the two behaviors aren't really the same.
What do you think is the difference between whining and complaining?

Whiners are inwardly focused. They want things to be different, but they don't really know how it should happen. They feel unjustly burdened by the collective expectations of bosses and coworkers. But rather than focus on resolving specific problems, whiners search for general affirmation of their status as victims. They want sympathy and attention, rather than solutions.

Negative People

Whining is one of the least effective forms of protest, yet it's one of the most common forms of expression in the workplace.

Most people whine once in a while. Whining can relieve stress or help you blow off a little steam.

But continual whining irritates and annoys coworkers. They may ostracize the whiner, or worse, get caught up in competing with the whiner for attention.

You can recognize whiners from the way they express their negativity in the workplace.

Whiners use generalized, self-centered words like I, always, never, everyone, me, or nobody. Their message is one of self-pity – life is unfair, nobody listens, they're being treated poorly, and nobody appreciates what they do.

They also make use of superlatives, absolutes, and emphasizers – phrases like "the worst," "most awful," "absolutely cannot," or "so bad."

Rosalie works as a creative director at a large advertising and communications company. The nature of her work means she has to deal with many people in different departments. And because much of her work is project based, she depends on keeping positive relationships with coworkers. This is especially important for those people she depends on to help her meet project deadlines.

Rosalie often works with James, a copywriter. James has been known to indulge in whiny behavior. Follow along as Rosalie talks to James about their current project.

Rosalie: Hi, James. How's everything going? Did you get my notes about the new project?
Rosalie smiles

James: Yes, along with all the other correspondence everybody keeps piling on my desk. Nobody seems to care I have a full workload already.
James whines

Rosalie: Is there a specific problem?

James: It's just unfair that everyone expects me to do everything all the time. I'm only one person. I absolutely can't do what seems to be expected of me in one eight-hour day. It's so frustrating.

Rosalie: Well, the new project schedule is pretty important. I hope you'll go over my notes soon.

James: I swear, this is just the worst day ever. Everyone is after me, and I have a headache. The whole world seems to want a piece of James. You know?

Rosalie: Well, I'll check back with you a little later about those project notes.

James was demonstrating whining behavior. His comments were self-centered, and they were generalized and unfocused on any real solution to his perceived plight. Most tellingly, James demonstrated

Negative People

self-pity in an attempt to gain sympathy and attention from Rosalie.

32

Recognizing Complainers

The second common type of negative behavior is complaining. Complainers differ from whiners in that they're most often focused on specific issues or people. Complainers don't like to compromise. They often have a strong sense for how they think things should be, and any deviation from that produces complaints.

Complainers are easy to recognize because of the way they express negativity in the workplace.

They're usually the first to gripe about what's wrong and declare why things won't work. They put as much effort into finding fault as they do in dealing with issues. They love the word "but," as in "It's fine, but..."

Complainers often use phrases like "do it my way," "it would be better," "if only," "we've been through this," "I know what's wrong," or "you're wrong."

They may be genuinely trying to help but lack the communication skills to make things happen. Some have a particular image of the way things should be and a high level of frustration with any deviation.

But most often, complainers feel powerless to effect change, so they point out issues in the hope that someone else will take charge of fixing them.

Although you may find it tempting to dismiss them, you should always keep in mind that complainers can be valuable at times.

People who try to identify potential faults and problems can be an asset when you need critical thinking about ideas or issues.

But chronic complainers can unnerve and demoralize people who have to deal with them. Complainers rarely hold back from pointing out other people's shortcomings.

Complaining behavior annoys and alienates coworkers. It can cause them to become defensive and push back with complaints of their own.

Or they may get into the habit of ignoring or avoiding the complainer, meaning any good ideas, talents, or expertise the complainer possesses will be underutilized.

Rosalie is talking to Chantal, an accountant at the advertising and communications company where they both work. Rosalie has worked with Chantal before and knows she has a reputation for indulging in complaining behavior. Follow along as Rosalie discusses expense claims with Chantal.

Chantal: Hi, Rosalie. It's Chantal. I'm calling about the personal expense claims you submitted last week.

Rosalie: Hi, Chantal. I hadn't heard anything and I was wondering what was going on.

Chantal: Well, you could've called me. Anyway, I found something wrong. You didn't fill out the expense forms the way I requested.

Rosalie: Oh, what's the problem?

Chantal: Rosalie, we've been over this before, and you should know how I like to work. You should use a more readable font when printing out the document.

Rosalie: So my expenses are delayed because you didn't like the font I used?

Chantal: Yes, but that's not the point. It's not my job to fix things for you. This system runs smoothly as long as employees are careful and do things the way I say they should be done.

Rosalie: Yeah. We wouldn't want to panic the stockholders over a font issue.
Rosalie is slightly annoyed, but trying to lighten things up.

Chantal: Funny. But you still have to redo your expenses. The right way, this time.

Rosalie: Well, next time maybe you could get back to me sooner if there's a problem. Or better yet, send me an e-mail. Use any font you like.

Rosalie became annoyed by Chantal's inflexibility and dictatorial tone. Unfortunately, Rosalie reacted defensively by pushing back with a complaint of her own. She also took a step to avoid dealing directly with Chantal, by requesting the use of e-mail. This complaining-defensive cycle is detrimental to work relationships.

33

Recognizing Blamers

The third common type of negative behavior is blaming. Blamers avoid admitting their own mistakes and shortcomings by shifting the blame to someone or something else. Problems are rarely their fault. If blamers ever admit to having done something wrong, they'll justify it by claiming they were provoked. The blamer's automatic response is to "point the finger." By deflecting focus away from themselves, blamers avoid responsibility, often at the expense of coworkers.

Blamers have the worst qualities of whiners and complainers. They're often critical and judgmental, yet rarely offer any solutions to problems or issues.

If you don't deal with whining and complaining, these behaviors can escalate into blaming behavior. Whiners may indulge in blame if they're not getting the attention they seek. And like whiners, blamers often set themselves up as victims.

Complainers may become blamers when they think they're being ignored or their advice isn't followed.

Blamers also think they know where problems lie –
anywhere but with themselves.

Blaming is sometimes a defense mechanism.
Blamers may be trying to cover up incompetence or
may be genuinely afraid of responsibility. They use
blame to keep attention away from their own
weaknesses or inability to resolve issues. Other times
blame is offensive – used as a weapon to discredit
coworkers or to "get back" at someone who's blamed
them in the past.

You can often recognize blamers by their litany of
excuses:

- "I couldn't help it"
- "Everyone does it that way"
- "She told me to"
- "Someone else must have taken it"
- "If you wanted it that way, you should have said
  so," or
- "It's not my fault"

R osalie is talking to Vijay, a graphic designer,
about his input to an important advertising
campaign. Vijay has been known to use blaming
behavior. Follow along as Rosalie talks to Vijay about
designs for the project.

Rosalie: Vijay, have you got the revised designs for
the new advertising campaign? They were supposed
to be done today.

Vijay: I don't know anything about any design
revisions.

Working with Difficult People   105

Rosalie: The deadline is tomorrow. We discussed this at the last team meeting.

Vijay: I don't think that happened. Anyway, you should've sent me a memo if it was that important.

Rosalie: It would've been included in the action items on the minutes of the meeting.

Vijay: I don't think I got those minutes. Your assistant probably forgot to include me when he sent the minutes out.

Rosalie: He e-mailed the minutes out last week and I know you're on the list.

Vijay: The system must have had a glitch. That's why you should double check with people if you need something from them.

Rosalie: I need those designs by tomorrow, Vijay.

Vijay: You should have asked me earlier. Shelley and Andrew both have stuff they need from me today. If you think your work is more important than theirs, go tell them. You can't expect me to choose sides.

Rosalie: Vijay, we're going to miss the deadline if you don't get those revisions to me.

<u>Vijay:</u>   Now Rosalie, this is your problem, not mine. It wouldn't have happened if you were better organized. And if I may say, you're not going to get anywhere by being a bully.

Blamers shift responsibility away from themselves and rarely offer any solutions to issues that arise. When Rosalie asked Vijay about the work he was supposed to have done, he blamed Rosalie's assistant, the e-mail system, his coworkers, and Rosalie herself.

34

Recognizing Whiners & Complainers

In today's fast-paced, technically focused world, it's easy to forget that a workplace is made up of human beings with real and sometimes unpredictable emotions. Sometimes, these emotions can manifest in the form of negative behaviors such as whining, complaining, and blaming.

Reflect

Negative behaviors range from merely annoying to seriously destructive actions. So when is it appropriate for you to deal with someone else's negative behavior?

You'll often just have to put up with difficult people. But it's appropriate and imperative to deal with whiners, complainers, and blamers when their behavior is negatively affecting your work or the productivity of your team.

Your most important resources are the people you work with. So when the negative behavior of difficult coworkers impacts your productivity, you'll have to take action. But what can you do?

Difficult people don't change their behavior overnight. They don't change because you've confronted or shunned them, or just because you've told them to.

What makes them change is your positive, consistent, and solution-oriented approach to building and nurturing your work relationships.

When you deal with difficult coworkers, it's important to be a role model for how you want them to behave. Don't buy in to their negativity, and don't fall into the trap of competing with them.

You need to take a positive, proactive approach when dealing with difficult coworkers. Reflecting back negativity only escalates problem behavior. Select each negative behavior for more information.

Whining

Don't whine. This just affirms that whining behavior is acceptable. A positive and realistic approach shows whiny coworkers they aren't powerless to change what they don't like.

Complaining

Don't complain, at least not without proposing a solution to the problem. Being proactive shows your boss you have initiative. It also shows your coworkers that when you take ownership of an issue, you're on the road to solving it.

Blaming

Don't blame. Take responsibility for your actions instead of pointing at someone else. If an issue arises that's somebody else's fault, be constructive about how the problem can be resolved and prevented from happening in the future.

35

Dealing with Negativity

The main purpose of developing a strategy for dealing with negative people is to change the dynamics of their relationships with you. By following this strategy, you can encourage your coworkers to self-regulate their behavior and make working with them easier.

The strategy for dealing with negative people at work consists of three steps:

* listen to the person who's being negative
* demonstrate you understand the message, and
* try to resolve the issue

The three steps for dealing with negative people are the same when you're dealing with whiners, blamers, and complainers. But how you implement the third step is different when you're dealing with blamers. In this topic, you'll learn about how to use the three steps when you deal with whiners and complainers.

The first step for dealing with a negative person is to simply listen to what's being said. Listening helps you determine what type of negative behavior is being displayed and also whether what this person is saying has any intrinsic value.

Keep in mind it's easier to get people on your side if you give them a little of what they're seeking. Whiners are searching for attention; complainers want acknowledgement.

When you listen, it's important for you not to voice any judgment. At this point, it doesn't matter if the issues are true, valid, or relevant. By just listening to your coworker, you'll help create empathy and establish a base for your relationship.

After you've listened to your difficult coworker, the second step is to demonstrate an understanding of the issue.

You can do this by defining and summarizing the content and emotion of what your colleague has just relayed to you.

Because your goal is to head toward a better relationship, keep it friendly and positive. Speak to your coworker in the type of voice you'd like to listen to. Request affirmation or acknowledgement of your assessment of the issue. This will build trust so you can both move on to the third step.

Now that you've listened to your colleague and demonstrated you understood – but not necessarily agreed with – the message, it's time for the third step – resolving the issue.

For difficult coworkers, the issue is the problem – or problems – they're reacting to.

For you, it's the negative behaviors these problems stimulate in your coworkers – behaviors that will affect your ability to do your work.

It's not up to you to simply take over your colleague's problems. This would only validate the negative behavior. The purpose of this third step is to change your relationship with your coworker by eliminating the negative behavior and replacing it with another, more acceptable, behavior.

36

Dealing with Whiners & Complainers

In the first and second steps for dealing with negative people, you establish empathy and build trust with your negative coworkers. Now is the time to validate their right to resolve the issue on their own.

Implementing the third step – resolving the issues that stimulate negative behavior – is different for whiners and complainers than it is for blamers.

For both whiners and complainers, you'll need to ask gentle probing questions that refocus their attention on resolving issues.

You can tailor these questions based on the information you gather during the listening stage and the demonstrating understanding stage.

Each of your questions should have a purpose. Whiners need to be focused on the specifics of what's causing their negativity. Complainers need to be focused on coming up with solutions, rather than just pointing out problems.

You can phrase questions in many different ways to subtly suggest to your negative coworkers that they need to come up with their own problem-solving decisions:

- What specifically is the problem?
- What have you done to deal with the problem?
- Who could you speak to that might help?
- What's bothering you?
- What exactly did he do?
- What will you do about it?
- What's the solution to this issue?

If your coworkers continue to be negative, don't reward them with sympathy or attention. Shift the conversation and questions back to the issues at hand.

Sometimes you might find it difficult or impossible to make any progress changing the dynamics of your relationships.

Conflict resolution is often more effective when handled by an authoritative third party. You

Negative People

shouldn't be reluctant to follow proper business channels if your coworker's negative behavior continues.

If you find the negative behavior doesn't stop, document your concerns to the appropriate authority. Management will normally respond to this sort of issue quickly when you're clear about the negative impact on productivity.

R osalie works as a creative director at a large advertising and communications company. She recognizes that James, a copywriter, indulges in whiny behavior. Follow along as Rosalie goes through the three steps of dealing with negative people.

Rosalie: Hi, James. I'm checking back to find out how you've progressed with reading the project notes I left with you. I need your input so I can submit the report at the end of the week.

James: What a day this has been. My phone has been ringing off the hook. About those notes, I haven't gotten around to them yet.

Rosalie: Tell me what the problem is.

James: Problem? Oh, well I'm just really, really busy.

Rosalie: I'm listening.

James: Well, I've got several projects on the go right now. You know how it is. I'm working so hard I'm going to make myself ill.

Rosalie: Just so I understand, what you're saying is that you haven't read my notes because you feel you've been too busy with other projects. Am I understanding that correctly?

James: I guess so.

Rosalie: Which of the other projects have deadlines that are coming up this week?

James: Well, umm. None this week. But I'm really stressed right now, and I have a dentist appointment I have to get to.

Rosalie: Since our deadline needs to be met, what will help you get to reading the project notes today?

James: Well, I could ask Reception to hold my calls for an hour. But those people never listen to me.

Rosalie: Thanks, James. I appreciate the effort. I'll go with you and we'll get Reception to hold your calls while you read the project notes. I'll touch base tomorrow morning and get your input for my report. How's that for a plan?

James: It sounds doable.

Rosalie followed the three steps for dealing with negative people when she spoke to James. First, she listened to what he had to say to create some empathy in the relationship. Second, she demonstrated she understood his message by summarizing the issue. Third, she asked James a series of gentle probing questions to steer him away from the whining behavior and specify what could be done to resolve the issue.

By following the three steps for dealing with negative people, you'll impart a valuable message to your coworkers – negative behavior won't get them what they want. And you'll all benefit from positive and productive working relationships.

When you are dealing with whiners or complainers, step three is attempting to resolve the issue by asking a series of gentle probing questions. With whiners, you'll need to get them to focus on specifics, rather than letting them indulge in general lamentation. With complainers, you'll need to get them to focus on solutions, rather than just criticism.

37

Dealing with Blamers

Everyone makes mistakes. In fact, human error can occur in an almost infinite number of ways. But at work, individuals who are experienced and knowledgeable are expected to anticipate negative outcomes and avoid them. When workplace errors inevitably occur, employees have two choices: accept responsibility or play the "blame game."

Blamers share a common characteristic – they find it easier to attack a person or situation than to tackle a problem. But there isn't just one type of person who becomes a blamer.

A number of different causes can cause blaming behavior. Some people consider it a sign of weakness to accept responsibility, or they view any criticism as a personal attack.

Other people may be frightened to face what they've done because in the past they've suffered punishment for making mistakes.

Blamers may be protecting their egos or reputations. They may be bullies or the type of person who just can't admit they're wrong. At worst, they may be sly manipulators looking for opportunities to benefit at the expense of others – often looking for ways advance their own careers.

The three steps for dealing with negative people are the same for blamers as they are for other negative behaviors like whining and complaining:

- listen to the person who's being negative
- demonstrate you understand the message, and
- try to resolve the issue

The difference between dealing with whiners and complainers and dealing with blamers is in how you implement step three – resolving the issue.

Dealing with blamers is an essential workplace skill. When you work with other people, it's inevitable that someday you'll be blamed for something.

It may be something simple – you forgot to send a reminder about a meeting – or something major that can affect your career – your actions lost a client or caused an accident. And sometimes the blamers will be absolutely right.

How you resolve issues with blamers depends on whether the responsibility for the issue lies with you or with them. Select each responsibility for more information.

When you're at fault

When you're at fault, owning up to your responsibility is best. Acknowledge what the blamer is saying, and ask what you can do to help.

Once you take ownership of the issue, you can apologize, clarify what happened and why, seek a solution, and move on. It's important to make clear that you're more interested in resolving the issue than in being right.

When they're at fault

When blamers are at fault, you'll need to confront them. Blamers will usually stop their negative behavior when you give them specific examples of how their mistakes, miscalculations, or omissions caused the issue.

Don't be vague. Blamers find it difficult to shift the blame when you're precise.

Remember that blamers associate responsibility with negative consequences. They won't respond to an attack.

Be nonthreatening and diplomatic when you present your position. This will help blamers feel like it's safe to accept responsibility if they're wrong and will give them ownership in the solution if they're right.

It also helps to create empathy. For example, you might tell them about a time when you made a mistake, accepted responsibility, and moved on.

Using gentle, probing questions can help you steer blamers away from negative blaming behavior and toward positive problem solving. Keep your questions simple at first and make use of closed-ended questions. Don't give blamers the chance to reinterpret facts to create the impression that they were right all along – either in what they did or in blaming you.

R osalie is in the staff room of the advertising and communications company where she works as a creative director. She's just encountered her coworker, Vijay, who's upset with Rosalie because she's missed a meeting. Follow along as Rosalie deals with Vijay's blaming behavior.

Vijay: Rosalie, where were you this morning?
Vijay is annoyed.

Rosalie: This morning? I'm not sure I understand. Just tell me exactly what the problem is and I'll listen.
Rosalie is confused.

Vijay: I just got out of our 11:00 meeting with the clients. You were supposed to be there to help me with the presentation, but you didn't show up.
Vijay is visibly upset.

Rosalie: I thought that was tomorrow...
Rosalie is puzzled.

Vijay: You're wrong. It was changed. I sent you an e-mail about it. This is all your fault.
Vijay is still annoyed.

Rosalie: Vijay, you're absolutely right. I apologize. I forgot to make the change in my agenda.
Rosalie is apologetic.

Vijay: You made it really difficult for me. If this project falls apart, I'm going to make sure everyone knows whose fault it is.
Vijay is now starting to calm down a bit.

Rosalie: So are you saying the clients might be unhappy because you did the presentation alone?

Vijay: No. I didn't do anything wrong. I did fine, considering I had no help from you, even though you were supposed to be there.

Rosalie: So everything went well with the clients. The issue is that I wasn't there to support you?

Vijay: Yes.
  Vijay is now completely calm.

Rosalie realized she was at fault for missing the meeting with her clients. When Vijay confronted her about the issue, she dealt with his blaming behavior.

In step one, Rosalie listened to what Vijay had to say. In step two, she showed understanding by stating the issue and owning up to her mistake.

Rosalie was successful in the first two steps because she was proactive in her approach. She was diplomatic and nonthreatening, and she used closed-ended questions to steer Vijay away from his blaming behavior.

Rosalie has followed steps one and two for dealing with difficult people. Now it's time for step three — resolving the issue. Follow along as she deals with Vijay's blaming behavior.

Rosalie: I'm really glad you managed to handle things. Now let's talk about a solution to the issue. OK?

Vijay: Sure.

Rosalie: I want to prevent this from happening again. In the future, I'll make sure I put any schedule changes into my agenda immediately. I'll also give you my cell number so you can call me anytime. Is there anything that would help from your side of things?

Vijay: Well, I could use the automatic reminder feature on our in-house e-mail system. When you accept a tagged e-mail, I'll get a notification you've read it, and you'll get a series of reminders popping up on your computer screen until you acknowledge the change.

Rosalie: It sounds like we have a good solution. Thanks, Vijay. Well, I have to get back to my office. I'll see you at the team meeting tomorrow, and I promise you I'll be on time!

Vijay: I'll keep an eye out for you.

In the third step, Rosalie resolved the issue with Vijay by seeking a solution and then moving on. She was successful because she secured Vijay's trust and commitment by including him in a shared solution to the issue.

Dealing with a blamer

To deal with negative people, you follow three steps: listen to the person who's being negative, demonstrate you understand the message, and try to resolve the issue.

When dealing with blamers, you have two options for implementing step three – resolving the issue. When you're at fault, you should own up to your responsibility, acknowledge what the blamer is saying, and ask what you can do to help resolve the issue. When the blamer is at fault, you should confront that person with specific examples of the problem and then work together to resolve the issue.

Part VI

Procrastinators

Have you ever worked with someone whose desk is cluttered with files and papers? Their voice messages haven't been checked in days and their e-mail is still being forwarded to an old address. There are crumbs under their chair because they eat at their desk – too afraid they might encounter one of their coworkers if they heads for the lunch room. And, while you could look for them in their office, they will not be there. It's their anniversary and they had to leave work early to get a gift for their spouse before the stores close.

38

Types of Procrastinators

Procrastination is a behavior based on an inability or reluctance to prioritize decision making. It's a complex problem that leads to seemingly irrational behavior by the procrastinator – wanting one thing and then doing the opposite.

This is because, on a rational level, procrastinators understand and acknowledge that they have to take action to achieve their goals, but, on an emotional level, they resist making decisions that would propel them toward those goals.

Procrastinators may dislike their inability to accomplish their goals on time, but they don't change because their fear or anxiety is stronger than their ability to put things in perspective. But procrastinators can change their behavior if you know how to deal with them. This means developing a communication strategy that allows them to feel secure enough to think clearly about their priorities.

Being careful about decisions isn't a bad thing; in fact, it's responsible to consider the consequences of your actions. But at work, you're part of a social infrastructure – connected in some way to everyone else in the organization. And the inability or reluctance of procrastinators to make timely decisions can seriously affect your ability to do your job.

Reflect

*Think of a time when you didn't finish a task
on time. Why do you think that happened?*

Your reason for not completing a task on time is
likely as unique as the task itself. Maybe you were
faced with what you thought was an unreasonable
deadline.

Perhaps you lost interest in the task or found
something more interesting to focus on.

Or, possibly, you felt you needed extra time to do a
really good job.

It's human nature to avoid or put off completing
work from time to time. But sometimes delaying
finishing tasks becomes a serious behavior pattern –
procrastination.

It's important for people to have control over their
working lives, but it's also important that they be able
to work effectively with their coworkers.

Procrastinators often jeopardize their careers and
work relationships because of their failure to support
schedules or follow through on commitments.

But if procrastination is such a problem, why do
people fall into this behavior pattern?

Procrastination is triggered by anxiety that
interferes with an individual's capacity to complete
tasks in a timely fashion. This is known as avoidance
behavior. When people procrastinate, they choose
inaction over action because they want to avoid
something unpleasant. In short, procrastination is a
"quick fix" to relieve their anxiety.

The roots of procrastination are varied. Some people procrastinate because they fear they won't succeed in what they have to do.

Others use procrastination as a rebellion against authority. They fear a loss of power and control if they "do what they're told."

Still others have emotional attachments to their work and resist sharing or giving up influence.

Whatever the impetus for their behavior, procrastinators have one thing in common – they fear a loss of control over their actions and responsibilities.

But in a work environment, total control is impossible. So procrastinators rationalize that if they can't control what they have to do, they can at least control when they do it.

There are three common types of procrastinators you may encounter in the workplace – avoiders, storytellers, and perfectionists.

The avoider

Avoiders procrastinate by being noncommittal – they're good at disappearing from the radar when needed. And it can be a challenge getting them to answer a voice message or e-mail.

The storyteller

Storytellers procrastinate by telling you what they think you want to hear. They're experts at concocting a web of half-truths to cover up what's really happening.

The perfectionist

Perfectionists procrastinate by becoming entrenched in the details of their tasks. Of all the types of procrastinators, perfectionists are the most emotionally attached to their work.

39

Recognizing Avoiders

The avoider is one of the most common types of procrastinator. These procrastinators fear that they can't adequately handle or complete a task, and so they choose to avoid it. Avoiders are frustrating because they're aware of their responsibilities, but avoid any firm commitments to completing tasks. Avoiders are chronically indecisive. Thinking about the consequences of their actions causes them mental anguish. That's why they live in the present, in denial about impending deadlines.

Typically, avoiders hate confrontation and hate disappointing others. Due to the fear of not being able to deliver by their deadlines, they tend to avoid the people that are depending on them.

They go to great lengths to avoid encountering coworkers whom they fear they've let down, or will let down.

For example, they may hide out in their office, and neglect to answer their correspondence. Or they may call in sick to avoid having to explain why they can't submit their work.

Avoiders are also in denial about work relationships. They convince themselves that everyone is working well together, and they tend to concentrate only on what needs to be done to keep their heads above water.

If coworkers do manage to catch up with them, avoiders will evade answering any questions with specific answers. They like the word "maybe" and the phrase "I'll try."

Avoiders often ignore the fact that work isn't getting done, until they hit a crisis and have to put out a call for help. In fact, being rescued makes many avoiders feel valued.

C onsider Kiran, who works in management for a large printing and graphic design company. The company does work for a number of regular customers, but also works on special projects with certain clients.

Kiran has just met up with Jae, one of the junior sales managers at the company. Kiran has been trying to make contact with Jae for several days about a project he's proposed to a museum. Kiran suspects Jae's been intentionally avoiding her. Follow along as Kiran corners Jae.

Kiran: Jae! There you are. I've been looking for you.

Jae: Oh, were you?

Kiran: I left you several voicemails, and I sent you an e-mail. Look, I'm doing the scheduling for our upcoming projects, and I need to know if the museum has signed on for that art book project.

Jae: Oh, right. Well, everything's fine. Just fine.

Kiran: But I need to know if that project is a go, so I can schedule the other projects.

Jae: Absolutely, and I'll have to get right on that.

Kiran: When will I know if that project is happening or not?

Jae: Soon. Real soon. Anyway, I've got to run. Give me a call sometime and we'll work it all out.

Jae showed typical avoider behavior when Kiran confronted him about the museum project. Rather than tell Kiran he didn't have an answer, he put off responding to her phone or e-mail messages. When Kiran finally caught up with him in person, Jae avoided specifics by answering her questions with vague assurances.

40

Recognizing Storytellers

Another type of procrastinator is the storyteller. Storytellers are people-pleasers. Unlike avoiders, storytellers don't hide when they're facing a crisis. But rather than face your displeasure, they fabricate credible-sounding descriptions of their accomplishments and progress. Dealing with storytellers can be extremely frustrating because you never know what to believe when you're talking to them.

Storytellers are often disorganized and frequently overcommit themselves as they try to accommodate the desires of others.

They live in the moment and, in any situation, they're more concerned with accommodating you than considering the consequences of their behavior.

Storytellers tend to daydream rather than complete their work. They're often creative types, spinning pleasing stories out of half-truths and selective omissions, but not following through with any concrete plans for action.

M ike is a graphic artist who works with Kiran at the printing company. Kiran calls Mike to check with him about an overdue design. Follow along as Kiran experiences Mike's behavior.

Kiran: Mike, I'm looking for that print ad design you were preparing for the book launch next week. It's overdue.

Mike: It's fantastic. You'll just love it. I really put my heart into all the designs in this project because I knew it was important to you.

Kiran: Well, thanks, I guess. But where's the design? I have to proof it and get it to the newspaper today. You said it was done when I talked to you yesterday.

Mike: Right. Well, I sent it over to you through interoffice mail. Didn't it get to you?

Kiran: No. I wouldn't be here looking for the design if I had it, would I?

Mike: Kiran, you're so funny. I'd run you off another copy, but my computer corrupted the file. I guess we'll just have to wait and see if it turns up. I'm sure it will.

Kiran: Oh, OK. But time is really running short. Can I check back with you later?

Mike: I'll look forward to it.

Mike is a classic storyteller. Rather than admit he didn't have the design work done for Kiran, he changed the subject to something he thought would please her – the quality of the work. When Kiran questioned him about the whereabouts of the completed design, he came up with a plausible and classic excuse – it was lost in the mail.

41

Recognizing Perfectionists

A third type of procrastinator is the perfectionist. The priorities of perfectionists are based on what they would like to accomplish, rather than what's possible. They have an emotional attachment to their work, and don't feel a sense of accomplishment until they're completely finished. They make no allowance for the inevitable limitations and time constraints that are part of working toward a goal.

Perfectionists equate their work with their self-worth. In the past, they may have been rewarded for their attention to detail and self-imposed standards of perfection.

This has created a situation where they become absorbed in the minutiae of a task, at the expense of the big picture. They procrastinate because they fear making even the smallest mistake.

Perfectionists often run out of time because they don't prioritize.

Because they're aiming for perfection, every detail deserves their attention. Coming close is experienced the same way as failing.

For perfectionists, "good enough" is never good enough.

Perfectionists find it difficult to be part of a team. They're intolerant of colleagues whose standards don't measure up to their own, and fear that sharing or delegating tasks will mean a loss of control.

They rationalize to themselves that letting go of control means that others will let them down by producing less-than-perfect work.

M inette is a photographer who works with Kiran at the printing company. Follow along as Kiran stops by Minette's studio to pick up a series of photos for inclusion in a fine cooking magazine article.

Kiran: Hi Minette, I'm here to pick up the pictures for the cooking magazine article.

Minette: Sorry, they aren't done yet. They just didn't turn out how I wanted them. I'm reshooting tomorrow.

Kiran: But you knew the photos were due today. I have to get them over to the Graphic Design department so they can be incorporated into the magazine design. We're on a tight time line, and a second photo shoot isn't in the budget.

Minette: Kiran, do you just want it done? Or do you want it done right?

Kiran: I know you like things just so, but why don't you let me see what you have? Maybe those shots will be good enough for our purposes.

Minette: It's not your artistic reputation on the line. I don't let my work leave this studio unless it has my seal of approval.

Kiran: Minette, you're letting the team down.

Minette: Well, maybe you all need to aim a little higher.

Minette is demonstrating perfectionist behavior. Rather than check with Kiran, she made the decision to reshoot the pictures for the magazine, even though this would upset the schedule. When Kiran asked to see the work that had already been done, Minette refused. This showed the typical perfectionist rationalization that letting go of control means less-than-perfect work

42

Dealing with Procrastinators

Dianne is at a loss about how to work with her teammate Sandy. His chronic lateness, inability to follow through on commitments, and talent for disappearing just when he's needed most are difficult for everyone, but particularly for a super-organized person like Dianne. Despite Dianne's threats and recriminations, and Sandy's vows to change, the team has failed to meet important deadlines on a number of recent projects.

When you deal with procrastinators, it's easy to get caught up in a mutually frustrating cycle, just as Dianne did with Sandy.

What Dianne failed to realize was that when you work with procrastinators, your influence over them is limited. You can't shame or force them to cooperate or to comply with your wishes.

And because procrastinators aren't direct about what they're doing – or not doing – you may not even know something is wrong until you reach a crisis. This is followed by recriminations and promises to change – until the next time.

Reflect

What do you think your role should be when you're dealing with a procrastinator?

The biggest benefit of developing a strategy to deal effectively with procrastinators will be your ability to meet deadlines. Remember, as far as your work relationship is concerned, procrastinators don't have their priorities straight – they put perfection and emotional comfort, or placating others, above timeliness. When you have an effective strategy to help procrastinators realign their priorities, their behavior will no longer affect your ability to meet deadlines.

It's appropriate to deal with a procrastinating colleague when the behavior is impacting on your own work, or when you're responsible for supervising a time line.

But even with a strategy in place, you may still find it difficult or impossible to make any progress changing the dynamics of your relationship with a procrastinator.

In this situation, you shouldn't be reluctant to escalate the issue through proper business channels. If you find the procrastination doesn't stop, document the negative impact it's having on productivity. Management will normally respond quickly to this sort of issue.

Meeting Privately

The strategy for dealing with procrastinators involves four steps. First, arrange to meet privately to discuss the issue. Next, state the facts about the procrastination. Then, provide the procrastinator with positive reinforcement. Finally, help the procrastinator resolve the issue.

Step one in the strategy for dealing with procrastinators is to arrange to meet privately to discuss the issue.

When you approach your coworker about meeting with you, be careful not to point fingers. Despite the importance of openness and honesty, you need to keep in mind that the purpose of this meeting is to foster a smooth working relationship.

Coming across as abrasive or dictatorial will do your relationship more harm than good.

Make sure you choose an appropriate location for your meeting. This should always be somewhere private. You might humiliate or anger your coworker if you bring up your concerns in the hallway, on the elevator, or anywhere other people are present. You might ask your colleague to meet in your office, if you have one. Sometimes a neutral location, such as a conference room, is best. Neutral locations have the benefit of minimizing distractions, emotional triggers, and power struggles.

Meeting privately doesn't always mean meeting in person. If your colleague works from home, or if you're a member of a remote team, you could arrange a private phone call or an instant message (IM) conversation.

More casual approaches like a phone call or an IM conversation can be useful if your peer is comfortable with those methods of communication. Also, these may be the only way for some remote team members to have "real-time" contact.

K iran works in management for a large printing and graphic design company. An important part of her job is scheduling the human resources and production time for the company's projects.

Kiran has been faced with a number of issues caused by the procrastination behavior of Jae, a company sales representative. Most recently, Kiran missed a deadline because she had to rework a complicated schedule. This was due to one of Jae's clients canceling a project to launch a new magazine.

Kiran has determined Jae avoided telling her when the client canceled the project a few weeks earlier. She's decided it's time to take steps to deal with her colleague's procrastination.

Follow along as Kiran implements step one of her strategy for dealing with procrastinators – arranging to meet privately to discuss the issue.

Kiran: Hi, Jae. I was wondering when we could get together for a meeting.

Jae: A meeting? Is something wrong? I'm kind of busy doing stuff.

Kiran: I've had some issues with the resource scheduling for our projects. I'd like to discuss the part you could play in helping me do that efficiently.

Jae: Oh, yeah sure. We can meet sometime.

Kiran: I've booked the conference room for today at 2:00. Is that good for you?

Jae: Oh, I might be busy.

Kiran: Well, we could meet now since you're in.

Jae: No, no. 2:00 is fine.

Kiran: Great. I'll meet you in the conference room at 2:00.

Kiran correctly implemented step one in her strategy for dealing with a procrastinator. She contacted Jae and arranged to meet him in a private and neutral location. She laid the foundation for a smooth working relationship by being polite and diplomatic in negotiating the meeting. She also resisted the temptation to lay blame, even though Jae had caused her scheduling issues.

Stating the facts

Step two in the strategy for dealing with procrastinators is to state the facts about the procrastination issue. During this step, you objectively lay out the facts of exactly how your coworker's behavior has affected your ability to do your job.

Your approach to stating the facts may be different if you're going to be working with procrastinators on a project, rather than if you work with them in an ongoing capacity.

If you find out you're going to be working with someone you know, or whose "reputation precedes them," you might anticipate problems with procrastination.

In this case, rather than wait for an issue to arise, you could ask to meet the procrastinator at the beginning of the project, and state the facts by projecting the consequences of failing to meet deadlines.

When you meet with your procrastinating coworker, remember that your goal is to find a mutually acceptable solution through communication and cooperation.

Make sure you're diplomatic when you present your points, and above all, don't be critical, opinionated, or self-righteous.

You want to ensure the procrastinator will be open to you and willing to consider the case you're making for change.

Your approach to stating the facts should also be tailored to the type of procrastinator you're dealing with – avoiders, storytellers, or perfectionists.

Avoiders

Avoiders are afraid of the consequences of making a decision and cope by making no decision at all. You need to reassure avoiders that you won't get upset about the results of any decision they make.

Storytellers

Storytellers want to avoid relaying bad news, so they embellish the truth. You need to explain that giving you false expectations is more harmful than being forthright about being unable to meet a commitment.

Perfectionists

Perfectionists fear that making a decision will result in less-than-perfect results. You need to explain that you appreciate attention to detail but work that comes in late is far from perfect. You can help these people refocus their perfectionism on timeliness.

K iran is meeting with Jae in the company's conference room. Follow along as Kiran implements step two of her strategy – stating the facts about how Jae's procrastination has affected her.

Kiran: I appreciate you taking the time to meet with me, Jae. I wanted to talk to about an issue that arose out of the magazine project. You may not be aware of this but something you did had a negative effect on me. Would you be willing to talk it over?

Jae: Oh, well I guess so. Are you angry with me? What do you think I did?

Kiran: Jae, I just want to tell you how this issue affected me. I'm not here to lay blame, just to work things out with you.

Jae: OK. Go ahead.

Kiran: Thanks. Now, the magazine project was canceled several weeks ago, but you didn't tell me about it. Last week, I worked our spring printing and editorial schedule around the project and then I had to redo the whole thing.

Jae: I meant to tell you, but I thought you might be upset and think it was my fault the project didn't happen.

Kiran: My priorities are to get our projects scheduled efficiently and effectively. You can help me do that by letting me know right away when there's a change that affects the schedules. Don't worry about what I might think. We need to look forward, not back. Can we agree on that?

Jae: I understand what you're saying. If I'd told you right away, I'd have saved you a lot of rework. I feel bad about that.

Kiran: You should feel good that in future we'll be on the same page. No pun intended.

Kiran was correct in her implementation of step two in her strategy for dealing with Jae's procrastination.

She clearly and objectively stated the facts of how she was affected when Jae procrastinated in telling her the magazine project had been canceled.

Kiran recognized Jae was an avoider, so she made sure to reassure him that she wouldn't get upset when he had something unpleasant to tell her. Kiran also emphasized that their mutual priority should be efficient and effective project scheduling.

Providing positive reinforcement

Step three in the strategy for dealing with procrastinators is to provide positive reinforcement. Procrastination is a hard habit to break. Your colleagues will need your support and encouragement to help them readjust their priorities.

Avoiders

Avoiders are paralyzed because they're afraid of failure. The key is creating a safe environment for them to make decisions. Discussing past accomplishments can help because this reminds them that making decisions can be rewarding. You can help avoiders by sharing your own experiences and creating an empathetic bond. Once they trust you, avoiders will be more likely to make decisions, rather than avoid them.

Storytellers

Storytellers protect themselves from disapproval by trying to please other people. You need to help them understand that what would please you above all is the simple truth. It often helps to establish some easy points of agreement about what type of response you expect when you communicate with storytellers.

Perfectionists

Perfectionists prioritize perfection over all else. You can support them by using "what if" scenarios –

exercises that evaluate possible outcomes and consequences. This helps perfectionists refocus on what a mutually acceptable outcome could be.

You should start providing positive reinforcement when you meet with your coworker, and it should continue from that point forward.

When you work with a procrastinator in a functional capacity, reinforcement should be an important part of your ongoing work relationship.

If you're working on a project, you need to provide positive reinforcement before a project starts, during the project, and afterward to help procrastinators stay on track.

Keep in mind that positive reinforcement isn't just simple praise. Your actions must relate directly to your work experiences. Your aim isn't to be critical but to show your coworkers you recognize what they're doing right and that you appreciate it.

Follow along as Kiran implements step three of her strategy – providing positive reinforcement to deal with Jae's procrastination.

Kiran: Let's talk about how we're going to communicate about our work so we both understand each other. What I need is for you to be straightforward with me when I ask you something, and for you to get information to me as soon as possible, even if it's bad news.

Jae: I just don't want you to be upset.

Kiran: I understand, Jae. It's easy to put off unpleasant decisions. Last week I had to reschedule one of our print jobs because I'd double-booked the presses. The client was upset, but at least he had time to consider his options. He would've been a lot angrier if I'd waited to tell him.

Jae: I heard about that. He managed to work around the delay, and we didn't lose him as a client.

Kiran: And remember last year when you got a sales award for landing that large government contract?

Jae: Right, I really had to pursue that client. If I'd procrastinated communication, another company might have won the contract instead.

Kiran: You're right. And I trust you'll use that same initiative when we're working together.

Kiran did well when she implemented step three of her strategy for dealing with Jae's procrastination.

She provided Jae with positive reinforcement by sharing her own experience in communicating bad news. She also reinforced positive behavior by talking to Jae about a situation where he had done well in the past by being persistent.

Kiran realized it was important to show Jae she recognized and appreciated his ability to make decisions.

Resolving the issue

The fourth step for dealing with procrastinators is to work with them to resolve the issue. Once you've discussed the procrastination issue and established a positive rapport with your coworker, you need to move quickly into problem solving.

This is the time to move the discussion toward resolving the procrastination issue you've raised.

At this stage, your approach to resolving the issue should be to secure procrastinators' commitment to changing their behavior, and then offer them your support.

Secure commitment

In the end, you'll need to help procrastinators be realistic about what needs to be done. As they will always attempt to put things off for as long as possible, the most effective approach is to ask them specific questions that steer them toward making a firm commitment to change.

Offer support

Procrastinators tend to be vague about the steps they need to take to complete tasks and reach their goals. You can offer to support them by helping them break down a task into a series of steps that build toward the final goal. You could also offer your support by arranging to check in with them on occasion so they can update you on their progress.

F ollow along as Kiran provides positive reinforcement. First, Kiran secures a commitment from Jae. Then, she offers Jae her support to help resolve his procrastination issue.

Kiran: Jae, I'd like to get your commitment to working with me in an open and transparent way from now on. Can I count on you?

Jae: Yes.

Kiran: So when I ask you a question, or if you hear something I should know, you'll get the information to me right away. And I promise I won't respond negatively. Are we in agreement?

Jae: I'll try, but sometimes things just get away from me.

Kiran: I'd like for us to check in with each other every few days. It'll just take a few minutes, and you can update me on your progress and what you're planning. That way we can both work toward the same goal – efficient and accurate schedules.

Jae: Sure, that'll keep my clients happy too.

Kiran effectively implemented step four of her strategy for dealing with Jae's procrastination. She secured his commitment to avoiding procrastination when he dealt with her. She also arranged to make contact with Jae on a regular basis. This will help Jae manage his work responsibilities and will allow Kiran to follow up with positive reinforcement when he meets his goals and objectives.

You won't be able to resolve every procrastination issue with one meeting. However, it's the beginning of working out an effective and efficient relationship with your procrastinating colleagues.

43

Procrastinators in the Workplace

Working with procrastinators can be an exercise in frustration. You end up doing extra work because they didn't do what they promised. You go through emotional turmoil when you have to cover for them. And you risk your own integrity when your team's rushed or incomplete work falls below acceptable standards. Clearly, it's essential that you have a strategy for dealing with procrastinators in the workplace.

The strategic approach to dealing with procrastinators has four steps:

1) meet privately to discuss the issue
2) state the facts about the procrastination issue
3) provide the procrastinator with positive reinforcement, and
4) help the procrastinator resolve the issue

K iran is a manager at a large printing and graphic design company. She is responsible for scheduling the human resources and production time for the company's projects.

Kiran works closely with Minette, one of the staff photographers. On a number of occasions, Kiran has been faced with production delays and cost overruns because Minette has been late turning in photographs. Recently, she was a week behind schedule handing in her photographs for a cooking magazine.

Kiran has decided to deal with Minette's procrastination. She's contacted Minette and arranged to meet with her in a private office at the company.

Kiran and Minette are meeting privately at their workplace. Follow along as Kiran deals with Minette's procrastination.

Kiran: Minette, I wanted to talk to you about a few recent occasions when your work has been late or I haven't received it. I understand you want things to be perfect, but when I don't get your photos on time, it's far from perfect.

Minette: What do you mean?

Kiran: Let's consider the monthly cooking magazine. It has to be ready for the distributors on a certain date or they won't take it. That means I have to go ahead with the schedule whether I have your work or not.

Minette: You didn't use my photographs? But they were near perfect!

Kiran: They were beautiful. But I didn't get them until after we'd gone to press. I had to buy some stock photos from an online company for the article you were working on. The article would have been much more appealing with your work.

Minette: I'm sorry, I was concentrating too hard on the pictures, and not on the process of getting them published.

Kiran: Let's work together on the process from now on. I'll make sure to check in with you regularly to make sure you're on schedule, and you'll get me photographs that are as good as possible within the time line. Are we agreed?

Minette: We are. There's no point in perfect pictures that no one sees.

Kiran and Minette came to an understanding because Kiran successfully implemented her strategy for dealing with a procrastinator.

To deal with Minette's perfectionism, Kiran met with her privately, and told her the results of not following the schedule. Kiran provided Minette with positive reinforcement, getting her to admit that it would be better to have her work done on time so it could be published.

Finally, Kiran offered to help Minette to keep their agreement by checking in with her at manageable intervals.

Applying the strategic approach

Imagine that you work for an information technology company that develops specialized software systems for corporate customers. A national chain of health care facilities has contracted with the company to develop an automated invoicing system for their hospitals and pharmacies.

Your responsibilities on the project will include quality testing of the new system. Meeting your project deadlines depends on timely delivery of the software from Dave, the team's programmer.

Although you like Dave, you're concerned about working with him. On your last project, your testing schedule was pushed back several times, even though Dave had assured you everything was on schedule. You anticipate this storytelling behavior might happen again, so you've decided to meet with him at the very beginning of this new project.

When arranging to meet to discuss the issue, it's important to keep it private so the participants can discuss issues freely, away from others. It can also be helpful to set the tone for the meeting by beginning to state the facts about the issue to be discussed.

Part VII

Manipulative People

The word "manipulation" means to manage or utilize skillfully. While this can be benign – in the sense of using your hands to manipulate a machine – in the workplace it can often have an interpretation that's more difficult to deal with. Manipulators in the workplace are those people who do whatever it takes to get what they want. They control or play upon others by artful, unfair, or insidious means, making others carry out their hidden agenda.

44

Types of Manipulative Behavior

Anyone in the workplace, from your coworker to your boss or your customer, could be a manipulative person.

Manipulative people have an arsenal of different forms of mind games to try to get what they want, maintain a grip on power, or remove something – or someone – in their way.

Manipulative people can be annoying; worse yet, they can be spiteful and malicious. Either way, their words and actions can be detrimental to your well-being, as well as to your reputation and career.

One of the worst aspects of manipulation is that people who are being manipulated often don't realize what's going on. Manipulators are subtle, and use tactics that make it seem as though they are the ones being hurt, or that they're simply being caring.

And clever manipulators exploit everyone's hidden weaknesses and insecurities. They know what emotional buttons to push to get you to do what they want without you even being aware you're being exploited.

Dealing with manipulative people and difficult situations requires rational, not emotional, responses. There are constructive ways to defuse potentially explosive problems and create a positive atmosphere in the workplace.

45

Recognizing Manipulative People

Do you work with someone who is always meddling in everyone else's business? Maybe it's a nosy coworker who likes to interfere. Or maybe it's someone who instigates trouble, manipulating people and situations. Such people can be simply annoying, or they can even be spiteful and malicious.

Manipulative behaviors include threatening you, flattering you, making you feel guilty, or putting you down. Some manipulators display confusing behavior by alternating between being overly affectionate and charming and then being cold or angry.

Manipulators thrive on getting others to unknowingly act out the manipulators' agenda. Being able to recognize manipulators in the workplace is vital to your career and your reputation.

Have you ever had to work with a friend who thinks another coworker is stealing his ideas and taking credit for work he did. The other coworker denies everything and even tries to convince your friend that he's the crazy one.

Manipulative people are generally subtle. When behaviors are hidden — as they are with most manipulators — you know something is wrong, but you can't pinpoint it.

And, if you don't know what's really going on, it can make you feel as though you're the one at fault. So, being able to recognize manipulative people in the workplace is important for your emotional health.

46

Categories of Manipulative Behavior

Manipulative behavior isn't always easy to recognize, and manipulators don't often admit to their own controlling behavior. There are, however, some habitual behaviors that manipulative people engage in. Once you have a better understanding of these behaviors, you'll be able to recognize them and use strategies to deal with them.

Manipulators are driven to control things. They may be motivated by boredom in their personal or professional lives, or feel threatened by coworkers or their work situation.

Or they may simply be unhappy, since being petty and vindictive are often symptoms of insecurity or unhappiness.

However, manipulators may have good intentions – by meddling to try to help out – or they may be blatantly confrontational.

S ome people manipulate from the sidelines, inciting you to get yourself in trouble. For example, Tanya wanted to take the lead on a software project for her boss, Bob. But Taku told Tanya he overheard Bob say he was giving that project to someone else.

In reality, all Taku overheard was Bob debating who to assign as project manager. But Taku wanted to see what would happen, so he exaggerated.

Tanya angrily confronted Bob because she felt she was being treated unfairly. She was penalized for jumping to conclusions, and Bob didn't appreciate being attacked. Taku incited the whole incident, but felt no repercussions.

Manipulators excel at controlling others. Their goal is to get you to do what they want, and they use many different tactics:

- withholding important information as a way of disempowering you
- acting angry, or punishing you by shutting down and refusing to communicate
- playing subtle mind games that keep you on your guard, and refusing to deal with conflict directly
- making you feel guilty by acting ignored, forgotten, hurt, wounded, unloved, or uncared for
- saying one thing and doing another, such as being pleasant to your face while talking viciously about you to others
- pretending to be victims by acting helpless in situations where they are in fact the perpetrators of the problem, and
- promising a change in behavior, without having any intentions of actually doing so

All the different tactics manipulators use can be grouped into four general areas. Types of manipulative behaviors include trying to deceive,

Manipulative People

demonstrating inappropriate emotion, attacking on a personal level, and diverting attention.

Trying to deceive

In addition to blatant lying, manipulators may try to deceive you by playing innocent, using outright denial, or playing dumb.

For instance, when one manipulator was called to task, she said "I was just trying to help, how could I know you'd get in trouble?"

Demonstrating inappropriate emotion

Most people dislike confrontation and strong emotion, especially in the workplace. Manipulators use this dislike to get their own way by demonstrating inappropriate emotion. They may cry or pout, or get angry and either shout or give you the silent treatment.

Attacking on a personal level

Moving a dispute from a professional level into a personal attack is a common behavior of manipulators. The goal is to take the focus off them and to provoke you into an emotional, reactive response so you'll do what they want.

Diverting attention

To divert attention, manipulators downplay their behavior and try to convince people that the behavior is not as bad as it seems. Some common ways of doing this are by rationalizing, using guilt, playing the victim, and minimizing their actions. They divert blame to another person, change the subject, or divert the conversation when the topic is about their behavior.

The first behavior – trying to deceive – seems the most straightforward. But it's not always easy to tell when a person is lying. Sometimes you don't know you've been lied to until it's too late.

Other times, the truth is clear when circumstances don't support the manipulator's story. But there are also subtle, covert ways to lie.

Manipulators may lie by withholding some of the truth from you or by distorting it. They may be vague and leave out important facts, in effect lying by omission.

Manipulators may lie by flat-out denial, refusing to admit they've done anything wrong and playing innocent.

Denial makes the victims feel unjustified. It's a maneuver used to make others back down or even feel guilty.

Another way manipulators lie is by "playing dumb," or acting oblivious. This form of lying is exemplified by "I don't want to hear it" behavior. Using this tactic, manipulators can avoid paying attention to their controlling behaviors.

A s an example of lying, consider Lauren's situation. Lauren is a project manager who has a manipulative coworker, Raj. She's trying to rally support for a new project initiative and asks Raj to get all those in favor together for a meeting. He deliberately leaves Enzo off the list – even though Raj knows he would be interested – because Raj doesn't like Enzo. Raj lies when he tells Lauren that Enzo isn't interested.

The second category of manipulative behaviors is inappropriate emotional demonstrations. Examples of these outbursts include temper tantrums, tears, or displays of grief that are used habitually to manipulate other people. Temper tantrums are usually intended to intimidate you so that you will back off, and tears or grief are intended to make you refrain from upsetting the alleged victim even further.

The third category is one of the most emotional for any manipulator's victim – personal attacks. Personal attacks try to make the victim the cause of the issue.

With this tactic, manipulators usually raise their voices and use aggressive "you" statements. They try to establish you as the root cause of any problems. If you play the manipulator's game, you end up in a fight without even knowing how it started.

Personal attacks are used to put you on the defensive. Using a combination of anger and guilt, many attacks begin with statements such as "Why do you always...", "Do you really expect me to...", "I can't believe you would...", or "How could you...".

Remember Lauren and her coworker, Raj? Lauren found out that Raj hadn't invited Enzo to the meeting, even though he knew Enzo was interested in attending. Follow along as Lauren asks Raj about it.

Lauren: I ran into Enzo, and he was disappointed not to be included at the meeting.

Raj: Oh, that's completely unfair, he's totally out of line, as usual!
Raj says angrily.

Lauren: Now Raj, calm down. I know you don't really care for Enzo, but just let me finish.
Lauren says worriedly.

Raj: How dare you check up on my work behind my back? Why should I have to justify myself, when everyone knows you're the one in over her head with this initiative?
Raj says angrily.

The first three categories fit into the manipulators' need to do whatever is necessary to follow their own agenda. The last category – diverting attention – more often comes in to play after manipulative behavior is called out. Manipulators create diversions to try to downplay their behavior, and convince people the behavior is not as bad as it seems. Manipulators divert attention by blaming another person or by changing the subject.

Manipulators use distraction and diversion techniques to keep the focus off their behavior. Some common ways of diverting attention are by rationalizing, using guilt, playing the victim, and minimizing their actions.

Rationalization can be very effective for manipulators, especially when the explanation makes just enough sense that a reasonable person could accept it.

After all, if manipulators can convince you they're justified in their actions – or that their actions are no big deal – they can pursue their hidden agendas without interference.

Playing the victim is a diversionary technique that manipulators use to gain sympathy and evoke compassion. The tactic is simple – convince someone that you're suffering, and they try to relieve your distress.

Attempting to evoke guilt ties in to the victim role, and usually refers to a shared history. Manipulators bring up previous actions and imply that you're uncaring, unfair, or ungrateful for not giving in to them now.

The subtext of appeals to guilt is typically "Because I did this for you, you should do this for me now."

Reflect

Have you ever been in a situation where someone tried to manipulate you through guilt? What kinds of statements did the person use?

F ollow along as coworkers Lauren and Raj further discuss Raj's slight against Enzo.

Lauren: Enzo is interested in the new project initiative. You should've invited him to the meeting even though you two don't get along.

Raj: Really? So you don't care that he insults me all the time? I would've thought that after I helped you last year, you'd stand by me. I guess I learned a hard lesson today.
Raj says sadly

Raj tried to divert attention from his actions by making Lauren feel guilty when he refers to a time in the past when he helped her.

He also played the victim by trying to elicit sympathy about an alleged insult.

47

Dealing with Manipulators

Not knowing how to handle manipulative people at work can impact many areas. You may feel you have no control over your life, and there may be low morale in the workplace. Your energy and productivity are often spent on worrying about the manipulative people instead of on your work. All the wondering about what they'll do next can make you feel like you don't have the right coping skills to deal with their behavior. But it doesn't have to be that way.

Some people like being manipulators. They might try to instigate trouble, by doing things like spreading lies about coworkers to destroy their reputations, or they might simply play the victim to get sympathy or pawn off their own work. When acts of treachery and betrayal such as these are tolerated because the target of manipulation won't confront the manipulator, bad behavior is likely to escalate.

If manipulators are never confronted, they will continue to target people. Manipulative people thrive on controlling the emotions and actions of others. That's what gives them power.

But if you can show them you won't be controlled, they'll lose some of that power. If you challenge their power, they may even stop the behavior on their own. But if you don't assert yourself and say no to manipulators, you're just another victim.

So, how can you confront a manipulator without setting yourself up for further attack? How can you convert such a person into an ally – or at least find a way to keep yourself out of manipulative games?

In general, when dealing with manipulative people, along with "don'ts," there are important "dos" to keep in mind:

- Do set healthy boundaries. You need to distance yourself emotionally in order to avoid getting caught up in the manipulative comments and behaviors. Cultivate detachment.
- Do document your interactions. These records can be useful later on in a confrontation or if you need

to make a formal complaint about the manipulator's behavior.

48

Dealing with Manipulative Behavior

While these general dos and don'ts are good to keep in mind, there are also five specific steps you can take to deal with a manipulator. When you decide to confront someone who is trying to manipulate you, first make sure you meet privately. Second, gently confront the person, and then, as the third step, explain that the behavior is unacceptable. Fourth, outline your expectations for future behavior, and finally, state the consequences if those expectations aren't met.

The first step is to meet privately to discuss the matter. A positive outcome to the confrontation is more likely if you don't humiliate the person by discussing it in public.

Try to find a private but somewhat informal or neutral environment. Non-neutral environments include standing in front of a large group of people or, if you are the person's manager, sitting across from your desk.

You should speak calmly when you ask to see your coworker. For example, you might say, "I need to talk to you about a problem. Do you have a few minutes? We could meet in the planning room, which is free right now."

Once you and the manipulator get to a private area, the second step is to gently confront the person. If you stay silent, you implicitly condone the manipulator's behavior. Confronting manipulators lets them know you're not an easy mark. And making the other person aware that you know what's going on is often enough to stop the manipulation. Either way, the manipulator's power is reduced.

In a confrontation, you need to be calm and not let your emotions show. In a soft tone of voice, clearly explain the problem to your coworker.

Don't get pulled into arguing. Listen to what your coworker says, but then leave the situation alone. You may have to agree to disagree, since manipulators will usually try to convince you their actions are justified.

C onsider the example of Rosa and Raymond, who work in a software company on the same project team. Raymond has evidence that Rosa is withholding important information from him. She seems to enjoy the trouble this manipulation causes within their team, as well as between their team and other departments. After Raymond asks Rosa to meet with him privately, he gently confronts her about her behavior.

Follow along with Rosa and Raymond's conversation.

Raymond: Rosa, you said you gave my assistant that report I needed, but I never got it. Later on, I saw it sitting on your desk.
Raymond sounds calm.

Working with Difficult People   167

Rosa: Really? Well, maybe your assistant forgot it.
Rosa says, innocently.

Raymond: When I don't get the information I need from you, I miss my deadlines. This is a problem for our team and for the people waiting for our work. Was it your intention to withhold information from me?
Raymond says, calmly.

Rosa: Of course not!
Rosa sounds unhappy.

Raymond tactfully confronted Rosa when he clearly stated the problem. He didn't get drawn into an argument or get defensive when Rosa tried to shift the blame. He remained calm while telling Rosa the impact of her behavior, and made it clear he understood her motivation when he asked about her intentions.

After you've stated issues clearly and asked about the manipulator's intentions, wait for a response – the next move is the other person's. After this, the third step is explaining that the behavior is unacceptable. The manipulator may not intend to cause problems – or, at least, may not admit to such intentions – but either way, you need to make it clear that such behavior is not acceptable.

The most common responses you'll get to your questions about intentions will be excuses, arguments, and accusations. Manipulators try to divert attention and minimize the situation.

If the manipulator denies wanting to cause trouble – as often happens – you can put the person on notice without forcing an admission by saying "That's good, because I can't tolerate that."

If the manipulator does admit to causing the problem, you can then ask why. Either way, the third step in dealing with manipulative behaviors is to tell the person the behavior is not OK.

Once you've made it clear that the manipulative behavior is unacceptable, the fourth step is to outline your expectations for future behavior. Clearly define what behavior you want to see in the future. This includes asking the manipulator to do what you asked. Ask about the other person's level of commitment to changing the behavior. For example, you should ask something like, "Can I count on this behavior stopping?"

Regardless of whether the manipulator answers yes or no about committing to change – or even if the person agrees with you or not – the last step is to state the consequences if the behavior doesn't change.

Some manipulators will exhibit strong reluctance to committing to change. Or they will continue to argue with you about it, even in the late stages of your discussion.

Consequences will depend on the situation, of course, but could include bringing the issue up with the boss, asking for mediation from HR, or getting corroborative documentation to the appropriate people.

I n a hospital, two nurses – Jenna and Akira – are vying for position as head nurse. Jenna has been badmouthing Akira to the hospital administrator, Ramon.

Jenna told Ramon that Akira was late on several occasions. Although Akira hadn't had a chance to check in on those days, Jenna knew full well that Akira was in the hospital working on emergencies.

Akira asks Jenna to meet her in the surgical supply room, which is one of the few private areas available for a discussion.

Follow along as Akira talks to Jenna about the situation.

Akira: Jenna, I know you've told Ramon some things about me being late for work that aren't quite true. What are you trying to accomplish by this?
Akira says, calmly.

Jenna: Nothing. We were just talking and the subject of lateness came up.
Jenna says, defensively.

Akira: Well, you don't even have your facts straight. I've never been late, and you badmouthing me to the administrator isn't behavior I can tolerate.
Akira says, calmly.

Jenna: I don't think I did anything wrong, and you were late.
Jenna says, petulantly.

Akira: If you had asked me about it, I'd have told you that I was here working on emergencies before I got a chance to sign in. Talking about other people behind their backs is wrong. In the future, please don't do it. If you have a problem with me, talk to me first. Will you do that?
Akira remains calm.

Jenna: I can do that.
Jenna says, reluctantly.

Akira: That's good. If it happens again, I'll be forced to go to HR with all my documentation. They need to know what is and isn't true.
Akira says, with determination.

Akira handled the discussion with Jenna very well. She said what she was thinking, but she did it without threatening Jenna. First, she chose a private place to have the talk, which isn't easy in a busy hospital.

Then she confronted Jenna about the problem by simply stating it, bringing the behavior out in the open. Akira explained to Jenna that badmouthing other people is unacceptable.

She then outlined her expectation that Jenna would stop her manipulative behavior, and stated the consequences – delivering proof to HR – if the behavior continued. Akira followed the five steps, and did it in a way that wouldn't negatively impact her working relationship with Jenna.

49

Working with Manipulative People

Sometimes, it may seem like everyone wants something from you. Maybe your boss wants you to work longer hours, or your coworker wants you to ignore his poor work. Salespeople want you to buy something, and customers need your time. When you say yes, is it your choice, or is it because you were manipulated into it?

Throughout life, you'll encounter people who are controlling and manipulative. But you don't have to feel frustrated or powerless. You can regain control of your energy and time when you use the five basic steps to deal with a manipulative person. First, meet privately with the manipulator, then gently confront the person. Tell the person the behavior is unacceptable, outline your expectations for future behavior, and state what the consequences will be if the behavior doesn't change.

Manipulation may be attempted through a person trying to deceive you, demonstrating inappropriate emotion, attacking you on a personal level, or trying to divert attention. Many manipulators try to use guilt to get people to do what they want.

C onsider the situation Amrit is in. She works for an energy company as an accountant. One of her coworkers, Enrique, has recently had a hard time keeping up with his work.

Although they've never been particularly close, Enrique cornered Amrit one afternoon and told her all about his wife, who's recuperating from major surgery.

Then Enrique asked Amrit for what he described as a "favor." He wants her to finish up his accounts so he can go home early, and for her not to tell the boss about it. Enrique tells her he feels his personal circumstances warrant her help. He says he'd do the same for her. Amrit is flustered by the request and asks him for a little time to think about it.

After going back to her desk and thinking, Amrit realizes that if Enrique really needed the time off, he could go to the boss and ask for it through normal channels. She realizes he's trying to manipulate her into doing his work, and decides to confront him. Amrit goes to Enrique's cubicle and says "What you're asking just isn't right, and we need to talk about it."

Enrique agrees to talk to Amrit, but only if they go to an unused office where they can close the door. Follow along as Amrit talks to Enrique.

Amrit: Enrique, you seem to be trying to get me to do some of your work. Is that what you mean to do?
Amrit asks calmly.

Enrique: Well, I'm just trying to go home to my sick wife. I would think most people would be glad to help out in a situation like this.
Enrique says sadly.

Amrit: If you need to go home, you know you just have to talk to the boss. I do have sympathy for your situation, but using my feelings to try to get me to take over your work is just not acceptable.
Amrit says calmly.

Enrique: You know the boss isn't easy to talk to. I thought you'd help out.
Enrique whines.

Amrit: I'll do it this time, but you really should have gone through proper channels.
Amrit says with some irritation.

Enrique: Thank you!
Enrique exclaims smugly.

To effectively deal with Enrique's manipulative behavior, Amrit still needs to outline her expectations for the future. She could tell him "Of course I'll help you out whenever I can. But you have to talk to the boss first. Will you agree to that?" Then, whether he states his agreement or not, Amrit should tell Enrique what will happen if he tries to guilt her into covering for him again. She could simply say "If you don't go to the boss first, I will."

50

Practicing Handling Manipulators

To begin practicing how to handle someone who exhibits manipulative behaviors, consider this situation. You and Chantal work together in a software development firm. You two are the only people working in Technical Support, and you're both supposed to provide employees with hands-on and telephone support. But lately, you've been swamped with work because no one wants to deal with her.

It's important to meet with Chantal privately, and then to gently confront her by stating the problem and asking about her intentions.

Whether or not she means to be off-putting, you should tell her that the unapproachable behavior is not acceptable. Specifically outline how you expect her to behave in the future, and state the consequences if change doesn't happen.

If you follow all the steps, you can have a productive discussion with a manipulator, which is never an easy thing to accomplish. If you don't properly follow the steps, the person may feel attacked and react angrily, or not change the manipulative behavior.

Part VIII

Self-serving People

You can't always avoid difficult people. Most people are easy enough to get along with. But there are still enough manipulative, arrogant, nosy, and annoying people in any workplace to make it impractical to simply hide in the corner and try to work in peace. These people aren't going to go away, and you can't allow them to negatively impact your interactions. You have to learn how to effectively deal with them.

51

Arrogant People

Although it's human nature to be motivated by self-interest, some people take it to extremes. Their self-serving behavior ends up causing difficulties for other people in the workplace. Self-serving people come in many forms, but we will focus on two common types — arrogant people and busybodies.

Arrogant people

Arrogant people act as if they are better than everyone else. Based on a fundamental insecurity, their behavior tends toward diminishing others in an effort to make themselves feel more important.

Busybodies

Busybodies are the office gossips, and just about every office has at least one. Busybodies not only engage in gossip, they actively seek out information to pass on to others. In doing so, they hope to enhance their image.

To reduce the effects of self-serving people on your work life, you should begin by trying to understand them better. You need to learn what motivates them and recognize the characteristics of each type of behavior, so that you can then apply appropriate techniques.

52

Recognizing Arrogant Behavior

"Wow. I bet you never thought someone from your social background would ever have a job this good."

This sort of simultaneous boast and put-down is a hallmark of arrogant behavior. Arrogant people make statements, ask questions, and give you looks that manage to make you feel small and insignificant. They can make your work life miserable. Learning to deal with this type of person will make you feel better about yourself, allow you to be more productive, and make going to work a pleasure instead of a chore.

Reflect

Think about someone you know who is a competent and decisive individual that you would consider confident but not arrogant. How does this person behave when interacting with others?

In contrast to the behaviors of confident people you may have identified, arrogant people tend to be insecure. They're afraid that you'll expose them as the frauds they are.

Arrogant people try to position themselves above everyone else because fear of rejection is the foundation of their behavior. This fear of rejection causes them to overcompensate and motivates them to exaggerate their own worth in an overbearing way.

Arrogant people's feelings of insecurity may not even be warranted. They may in fact be as good, as or better at what they do than everybody else. But they aren't sure of that and so they overcompensate.

Rather than focusing on improving themselves, arrogant people concentrate on diminishing others. Arrogant people try to diminish others by showing disrespect through sighs, looks, tone, or the way questions are phrased. They always seem to be asking, "Why?" in a belittling manner. They may roll their eyes, make sarcastic observations, or make jokes at others' expense.

As a result of their insecurity, arrogant people crave attention. In discussions, they show off by doing a lot of talking and not much listening. They have little interest in what others have to say, so they often interrupt when other people are speaking. They tend to overpower other speakers, question the purpose of decisions, and dismiss ideas other than their own. Arrogant people tend to ask questions in such a way as to imply that the other person's knowledge, performance, or thinking is inadequate.

M arko is the chairman of a city budget committee that includes Nils and Bernice. Bernice is known for being arrogant. Follow along with the committee's deliberations to observe Bernice's behavior.

Nils: As you'll all notice in the proposal, I've suggested a new program for remodeling and updating all city buildings in the next five years.

Bernice: Great idea. And I suppose you're going to pay for that out of your own pocket?
Bernice says sarcastically.
Marko: How exactly would you fund that kind of initiative Nils?

Nils: Well, I have a few different ideas.
Nils says hesitantly.

Bernice: And I'll bet not one of them will actually cover the total cost, right?

Nils: Uh, well...no. But with a few cuts elsewhere, we might be able to cover the expense.

Bernice: I thought so...
Bernice says triumphantly.

Arrogant people often try to build themselves up by bragging. They like to lord their status, knowledge, money, and resources over you.

Bragging may be done in an indirect way. As arrogant people complain about particular troubles – troubles which are naturally much more impressive than yours – they may slip in a little bragging.

For example, have you ever heard someone say something like "I really love my luxury sports car, but you wouldn't believe how much effort it takes to maintain"? Clearly, that person is not really asking for sympathy but rather is trying to impress you.

Arrogant people constantly talk about their problems, speaking for the sake of sensationalism, and are always playing the victim. They compare every situation someone relates to them with something they've experienced. By measuring someone else's experiences against their own seemingly far more important stories or difficulties, they diminish the other person.

53

Dealing with Arrogant People

Arrogant people aren't likely to just go away. They need attention, and need to demonstrate their superiority over you in order to bolster their own confidence. You won't be able to ignore them, so you might as well deal with them and improve your time at work. If you could deal with their behaviors using a few simple steps, wouldn't that be time well spent?

There are some general do's and don'ts to consider when dealing with arrogant people.

Do be confident. If you know your own self-worth, believe in your abilities, and feel you are strong, intelligent, and valuable, arrogant people can't diminish you. Their ability to belittle you is determined by one person – you.

Your strongest asset when dealing with arrogant people is your confidence.

Stay true to yourself. Don't rise to the bait when an arrogant person tries to get to you. Giving in to the temptation to react to their put-downs and off-handed insults gives them exactly what they want – power over you. Instead, remain calm.

In addition to the things you should do, there are some things you should not do with an arrogant person.

Don't argue. Getting into a debate with an arrogant person is a no-win situation. You can't win because arrogant people really aren't interested in listening to what you have to say. While you are busy arguing the facts, they will be using sarcasm, derision, and every other tool in their arsenal to make you insecure in your point of view.

Don't get angry. Getting angry and losing control is what arrogant people want you to do. Once you've lost control of yourself, they're in control of the situation.

You can and should make the effort to deal with arrogant people affecting your work life and end their influence over you. A basic open-and-close approach to arrogant behavior uses three simple steps:

1) open up the discussion by immediately confronting the arrogant person about the behavior using an open-ended question
2) state your disapproval of the arrogant behavior, and
3) close the door on the conversation by moving on to other business, giving the arrogant person no chance to respond

Self-Serving People

The first step, using an open-ended question to confront, puts the arrogant person in the position of having to defend insulting or belittling behavior. Instead of using closed-ended questions, which can be answered quite simply, you might ask "What exactly did you mean by that?" or "Why are you rolling your eyes?" These questions require the person to explain in more detail. After asking an open-ended question, make sure to wait for a response.

Arrogant behavior is difficult and embarrassing to explain. When confronted, an arrogant person may try to backpedal and claim what was said was just a joke. Or the person may press on and attack further. Either way, it's awkward and difficult to paint oneself as a reasonable person after being insulting or rude.

The second step is to state your disapproval briefly and directly. Say something like "I don't think making fun of my suggestion is appropriate." You should also outline your expectations for future behavior such as "I'd like us to get through this meeting without further sarcasm." Doing this restores your control of the situation.

The final step is simply to move on. Don't engage in further debate.

By employing the first two steps, you've effectively neutralized the behavior. There's nothing to gain and everything to lose by continuing to discuss it.

R emember the budget committee meeting where Bernice arrogantly put down Nils' proposal for updating all city buildings? She sarcastically asked if Nils was going to pay for it himself and derided his suggestions as inadequate. Fortunately, Nils is a fairly confident person who understands how to use the three steps for dealing with arrogant behavior.

Follow along with the committee's deliberations to learn how Nils applied the appropriate steps for dealing with Bernice.

Bernice: I think it's dumb to even pursue this line of inquiry without a viable funding plan. Are we supposed to just wave our magic wand?

Nils: Bernice, what exactly do you expect to achieve with sarcasm and insults?

Bernice: Uh, I wasn't being insulting. I was just kidding around. I do think that the plan is kind of dumb, I mean...I don't exactly understand how you think it can work.

Nils: I don't think sarcasm is called for, and I'd appreciate it if you could refrain from calling my ideas "dumb."

Bernice: Well...sorry.
   Bernice says sheepishly.

Nils: Let's just get back to discussing the budget proposals. We have a lot of serious work to do here.

Nils dealt effectively with Bernice's arrogant behavior. He applied the three steps by first asking her to explain her behavior with an open-ended question.

As Bernice dismissed his concern as a joke and continued to press her attack, Nils expressed his disapproval, stating his expectation for future behavior in the meeting.

When Bernice tried to discuss the issue further, Nils moved on, which helped negate Bernice's influence and take away her control of the situation.

Arrogant people are a fact of life. But once you understand that the root of their arrogant behavior is a basic fear of rejection, you can learn to deal with them.

In addition to generally refusing to lose your cool and engage in an angry debate, there are three distinct steps you can apply to help neutralize the impact of an arrogant person. You can ask for an explanation of the behavior, express your disapproval, and then move on.

54

Recognizing Busybodies

Busybodies are the office gossips. Their primary goal in life seems to be uncovering information no one else has and passing it on. Busybodies need to feel important, and they get that feeling when they appear to know things before anyone else does.

No secret is safe when a busybody is around. For that reason – and many more, including their effects on morale and productivity – you need to learn to identify the busybodies in your workplace and become skilled at dealing with them.

If someone begins a statement by saying, "I really shouldn't be telling you this, but...", then chances are you've found your workplace busybody. And, with an opening like that, it can be tempting to join in by listening further and engaging in gossip yourself. But remember, a busybody is unlikely to keep a confidence, so anything you say to that person will probably soon be public knowledge. And do you really want to be seen as a gossip yourself?

Miguel is the resident gossip at the small software company where he works. Recently, a few curious requests for information crossed his desk, and he started thinking. He decided they might indicate an upcoming merger with one of the company's competitors. The other day in conversation, he related his supposedly inside knowledge to one of his coworkers, exaggerating a bit along the way. By the end of the day, the entire office was in an uproar. Rumors were flying, people were upset, and arguments were breaking out.

The results of Miguel's rumor mongering included lost productivity, wasted time, low morale, hurt feelings, divisiveness, and increased anxiety among employees. He was in line for a promotion, but now Miguel's chances for advancement aren't looking good. His boss found out he started the rumor and she no longer trusts him with information. She thinks he's unprofessional and can't understand why he would do it. Why was he compelled to stick his nose in everyone

Self-Serving People

else's business? The answer is simple. Miguel is a busybody.

Reflect

You need to know who the busybodies in your workplace are before you become the victim of an untrue rumor. Recognizing busybodies begins with understanding what motivates them. What do you think motivates a busybody?

You may have correctly noted that busybodies often have low self-esteem. Spreading rumors and seeming knowledgeable makes them feel more important. People who engage in workplace gossip may also do it because they believe it will help them "fit in." They think sharing behind-the-scenes information with others will make them part of the group. Sadly, gossiping often has the opposite effect, instead lowering people's opinion of the gossiper.

Busybodies aren't simply people who talk about others. They actively pry into knowledge areas that are not their business. Busybodies dig up information and then present it to others in such a way that it makes them appear smarter for having known it.

Unlike legitimate distributors of information, busybodies don't use proper channels for spreading around what they know. They can't, because they aren't supposed to be privy to the information in the first place. So to get the word out, they use the informal methods of gossip and rumor.

C onsider the case of Martha and Boris. Boris often finds out early about new initiatives and changes to office policy by hanging out with Martha, the chief operating officer's assistant. Martha sends out all the company policy memos, so she knows a lot. As she sends out each e-mail memo, she's always glad to take a few minutes and explain any confusing language or complex procedures.

Boris passes on what he learns from Martha, being careful to never mention her name. Everyone in his department thinks Boris is really on the ball. They often go to him with questions about things they've heard through the grapevine, and he always seems to have inside information on what's happening.

But recently, Boris's coworkers discovered that he'd misinformed them. He'd speculated that the company was soon going to be converting to a new filing system. The chief operating officer is upset because people think there's a big change coming, despite his assurances to the contrary. He's asking around to determine the source of the rumor.

55

Dealing with Busybodies

There are some general tips that can help you deal with busybody behavior. These tips all fall under one general idea – "don't play the game."

You can begin to address busybody behavior by limiting your involvement with the people you identify as busybodies. You can't trust them not to reveal your secrets, so why would you want to associate with them any more than you have to?

Think about it. Do you really want to be known as the person who hangs around with the office gossip?

It's very easy to get drawn into the gossip habit and it can be hard to resist the lure of having inside information.

But you can discourage busybody behavior by refusing to participate. Don't let yourself spread gossip.

Communication is a two-way street, and so is gossip. Busybodies can't exist without an audience, so deny them one. Don't listen to gossip.

Let your coworkers know directly that you aren't interested in participating in gossip. You don't have to be judgmental – just say that you're not comfortable with the idea. For example, you could say, "I don't like talking about things when I don't have all the facts" and then excuse yourself from the conversation. Walking away from a gossip situation sends the message to everyone involved that spreading rumors is not acceptable. Others may even follow your example.

When you have to address a specific problem with a busybody, there are four basic steps to follow:

1) ask the busybody why they think the information should be spread around the office

2) let the busybody know that you're uncomfortable with the gossip
3) suggest to the busybody that you both go and talk to the person who's being gossiped about - the subject of the gossip, and
4) remind the busybody of the consequences of workplace gossip

Step 1: Ask why

Start by confronting the busybody and asking why the person thinks the information in question should be spread around and why it's appropriate for that person to do so. There's no excuse for betraying confidences and sticking your nose where it doesn't belong, so the busybody will probably have difficulty trying to explain the reasoning behind the act.

Step 2: Disapprove

The second step is to express your disapproval, regardless of whether or not the busybody tries to defend the behavior. Let the busybody know you don't approve of disseminating private or sensitive information.

Step 3: Suggest talking to subject of gossip

In the third step, you can drive home the point about the inappropriateness of the behavior by suggesting that you both go speak to the subject of the rumor and see what that person thinks. It's unlikely that the busybody will take you up on this suggestion.

Step 4: Remind of consequences

As a final step, remind the busybody there are consequences for spreading gossip and rumors. If your workplace has a specific policy regarding the spreading of gossip and confidential information, point that out to the busybody.

N ico is the assistant to the president of a bank. One of her colleagues, Hans, is the office gossip. He's always fishing for information about things that aren't related to his job. Recently, he started a rumor that the loans department would be downsizing by 20% in the next quarter. Nico doesn't know where Hans got this idea, and as far as she knows, it's groundless. But, true or false, she decides to deal with it before morale is affected.

Follow along as Nico uses the four steps to deal with Hans and his busybody behavior.

Nico: So Hans, Jenny tells me that you're the source of the information that's going around about the loan department downsizing. Is that true?

Hans: That's right. I hear it's going to be about 20%.

Nico: Well, I have no real knowledge either way, but I'm pretty sure the executive board didn't confide in you and ask you to spread information like this. Why are you getting everyone upset with your speculation?

Working with Difficult People

Are you trying to scare everyone into looking for new jobs?

Hans: Well, no. I just heard about some meetings that were taking place on the subject and put two and two together. I think people want to know about these things.

Nico: I don't think spreading your speculations around as if they were facts is right. As assistants, we're expected to be discrete.

Follow along with the conversation as Nico continues to confront Hans about his busybody behavior using the final two steps.

Nico: People will naturally assume this information came from your boss. Let's go ask her if it's OK to be talking about this. Maybe she can provide some clarification on the company's future plans.
Hans: Ah...well, let's not. She wouldn't be too happy about it.
Hans says nervously.

Nico: All right. But keep in mind the memo the president circulated last month on confidential information. I think it applies to this sort of gossip. If he knew about this, you'd probably be officially reprimanded.

Hans: I see what you mean.

Nico effectively applied the four steps for dealing with a busybody. She confronted Hans about his gossiping and asked why he thought he was right to be spreading rumors.

Nico followed that with an expression of her disapproval and a suggestion that they bring the issue out into the open. She suggested asking the person most affected by the gossip, in this case Hans's boss, to weigh in.

Finally, she gently reminded Hans that their company has a documented policy on the subject of workplace confidentiality and his behavior could have official consequences.

56

Dealing with Self-serving People

People use a variety of behaviors to get what they want. Although self-serving people come in many forms, two common types – arrogant people and busybodies – can be dealt with effectively if you use the appropriate strategies. First, you need to recognize which type of behavior you are dealing with, and then apply the correct steps.

C onsider the case of Paulo and Jameeka. They are on the same committee charged with developing the corporate goals for the coming year. Paulo came into the latest meeting with an aggressive attitude. He had already decided on the four primary goals he would agree to. After presenting his ideas, Paulo pushes for a vote. But the committee chairman suggests they put off voting until more ideas are presented.

As other members chime in with their proposed goals, Paulo often interrupts and shoots holes in their proposals in a derisive way.

Even when he isn't talking, he's rolling his eyes, sighing, and generally indicating through his body language his total disregard for what everyone else has to say.

At the end of the meeting, Jameeka is frustrated and angry at Paulo, and at herself. Instead of standing up for her ideas, she held back her comments and withdrew from the discussion for fear of ridicule.

As the meeting ends, Jameeka tries to address Paulo's behavior. She walks right up to him and lets him know what she's feeling. Follow along with their conversation to learn how Jameeka deals with Paulo.

Jameeka: Paulo, your behavior was demeaning toward everyone and my feelings were hurt.

Paulo: Well, I'm sorry, but all I did was present another side to the argument.

Jameeka: You ridiculed each idea presented. After a while, most people who wanted to speak up and put ideas forth, didn't – including me.

Paulo: If your ideas are so good, they should stand up under pressure. I think it's better that the weaker ideas don't get put forth.

Jameeka: That's no way to encourage creativity. In the future, could you try being a little more encouraging and less derisive?

Paulo: I don't really see the need.
Paulo says dismissively.

Jameeka: You really are an arrogant jerk!
Jameeka says angrily.

Paulo exhibits the classic signs of a busybody. He seems to be happiest when he's prying into areas that aren't his concern. He likes to spread inside information, even when it's someone else's personal business.

But busybodies can be stopped by appropriate use of the four steps: asking for the person's reasoning, indicating your disapproval, suggesting talking to the subject, and reminding the person about potential consequences.

When you apply the steps correctly, you can help Paulo examine – and hopefully change – his negative behavior.

Part IX

Micromanagers

Working with micromanagers can be annoying. It's almost certainly frustrating and time-consuming, and typically results in a loss of productivity. It's important to learn how to effectively deal with micromanagers in order to minimize the negative impact on productivity.

57

Understanding Micromanagers

Johan is typically a confident, capable employee. However, his coworker, Alan, has been looking over his shoulder constantly, questioning everything he does and offering endless advice. Johan is trying to take it in stride, but he's beginning to doubt his abilities and resent Alan.

Alan's behavior is typical of a micromanager. "Micromanager" is a term used to describe individuals who assert control by involving themselves in the details – no matter how minute – of their work and the work of others.

Need control

Key to the micromanager's behavior is the need to be in control, which stems from a general distrust and lack of confidence in the abilities of others. Micromanagers' need to be in control compels them to constantly seek updates and give input about the work others are responsible for. Essentially, fear of losing control prevents micromanagers from successfully sharing responsibility for work tasks.

Negatively impact productivity

Micromanagers meddle so much that it negatively impacts overall productivity. They involve themselves in so many things that they slow down the progression of work tasks.

Micromanagers often suffer from having a poor self-image, don't trust others, and need to be needed. They often tend to be anxious, suspicious, and inefficient.

Changing the micromanager's behavior is unlikely, so you're better off learning how to deal with this person. Adjusting your expectations and your approach to the micromanaging coworker can help you minimize the negative impact of the micromanaging behavior.

58

Recognizing micromanagers

Lily walks into your office and asks to know what your plan of attack is for a task you've been assigned. This is the second time she's been in today to find out how you're progressing. Before she leaves, she asks if you can provide an update before you go home.

Is Lily a micromanager? The answer is partly influenced by Lily's relationship to you. If Lily is your manager and you're working on a task that requires a lot of support, perhaps she's just doing her job. But if Lily is your coworker, then she could very well be trying to micromanage your work.

It can be difficult and uncomfortable to work with someone who wants to micromanage your tasks. The best approach is to preempt the behavior – plan for it, and be prepared to deal with the micromanager before the behavior starts. But before you can do that, you have to be able to recognize a micromanager.

Three indicators can help you determine whether your coworker is a micromanager. If the person tells you precisely how to do your work, expects updates more often than is productive, and presents a bottleneck to overall performance, you may be working with a micromanager.

Suppose you have a colleague who's constantly looking over your shoulder and telling you how to do your work – the first indicator of a micromanager. What do you suppose drives that behavior? For that colleague, it's likely all about control. In an effort to maintain a sense of control, micromanagers will tell you exactly what you need to do, when you need to have it done, and how you should do it.

C onsider Todd and Giselle, who work together. Even though they've both been assigned separate tasks, Todd keeps involving himself in Giselle's work.

Giselle is getting frustrated. She feels as though Todd doesn't trust her to do her job – he's constantly giving her direction about how to do her work and telling her when she should have it done.

Right now they're planning a silent auction – the organization's annual, charity fundraiser. Giselle has organized it for the last five years. This is Todd's first year. He's in charge of soliciting auction donations.

Follow along for an example of the micromanaging behavior Giselle routinely experiences when she works with Todd.

Todd: Giselle, please tell me you booked the venue for the silent auction.

Giselle: Yes, I booked it last year. The day after the auction, actually.

Todd: Oh, OK. Good thinking Giselle. I'd sure like to see you get the promotional work started. It would be a shame if the success of the auction was negatively impacted by a lack of timely promotion.

Giselle: I agree. That's why I've planned the promotional strategy and delegated tasks to experienced colleagues. We meet twice a week to make sure things are getting done as planned. You're welcome to join us, if you like.
Giselle says, pleasantly yet a little disgusted.

Todd: Perfect, I think I'll do that. One last thing, have you applied for the permit to sell liquor? I'd like that to be done by March 30th.

Giselle: Actually Todd, I plan to have that done by the end of this month because you need to apply a minimum of 45 days before the event. Otherwise you can't get the license.

The second indicator that a coworker is a micromanager is that the person expects updates more often than is productive. It's very frustrating when you find yourself doing more updating than actual work.

Remember Giselle? She's frustrated by Todd's continual requests for updates. The time she spends satisfying Todd's "need to know" is putting her behind schedule. She doesn't know how much more she can take without saying something she might regret.

Follow along to learn how Todd's requests for updates are affecting Giselle's work on the silent auction preparations.

Todd: Giselle, I thought I'd drop in to see how you made out changing the meal options. We talked about this yesterday and I haven't heard anything.

Giselle: Todd, I've taken care of the menu. I just didn't have time to let you know. I've been concentrating on doing the paper work for the liquor permit – it needs to be sent in today. This takes priority over giving you updates.

Todd: Well, all you have to do is send a quick e-mail. I just want to make sure the auction is a success. Perhaps you need to work on your time management skills.

Giselle: Really! Well maybe if you didn't ask for updates on everything I do, I'd have the time to do my work! In the last day you've asked for updates on three of my tasks. I think you've been in my office almost as much as I have. You need to back off.

The third indicator that you're dealing with a micromanager is when that person presents a bottleneck to performance. Such is the case with Todd and Giselle's team. On Monday morning, the team is meeting to discuss progress and projections for the week.

Unfortunately, this week's progress reports aren't good. Many projects – Giselle's included – are behind schedule because they're awaiting Todd's input, which he's insisted is necessary. Todd's micromanaging has created a bottleneck that impacts his and the team's productivity.

A micromanager can easily become overburdened and have a hard time keeping up with all the extra, unnecessary work.

59

Reasons For Micromanagement

The two most common reasons that individuals micromanage are inexperience and a lack of confidence in the abilities of others. Because micromanagement creates challenges to productivity, you need to work to build up the micromanager's confidence in you.

Individuals who are experienced in their roles may micromanage as a way of maintaining control. On the other hand, the uncertainty that comes with performing new or unfamiliar tasks can intensify a micromanager's need to be in control. However, micromanagement is likely to subside as the individual gains experience.

One way to address a micromanager's lack of confidence is to build the person's trust in you. Essentially, micromanagers don't trust others to do a good job. This absence of trust and need to be in control combine to produce this lack of confidence.

If you find yourself working with a micromanager, you can take some specific steps, in sequence, to build that individual's confidence in you: lay out your plan of action ahead of time to the micromanager; make any required changes to your plan; be dependable, and; update the micromanager frequently.

Step one is to lay out your plan of action ahead of time to the micromanager. This helps to demonstrate that you know what you're doing, that you're in control, and that you're paying attention to detail. Emulating the working style of the micromanager can give that person a sense of comfort and can help build trust and confidence.

Consider breaking your work into logical milestone deliverables that indicate how you'll get from the beginning of your work to the successful completion. Pay attention to detail, and include information about what, how, and when.

When you approach the micromanager, you may want to explain that, by developing this plan of action, you hope to ensure that you share a common understanding of what must be done. Or maybe mention that you value this person's input, explaining that, since your work together is contributing to one overall outcome, it's important to cooperate.

C onsider this example of two coworkers, Amelia and Charles. Working with Charles is difficult because he's a micromanager. Amelia decides to change her approach to working with him. The first thing she does is create a detailed plan of the work she needs to do. Once it's finished, Amelia e-mails him the plan. She's included milestones, as well as a step-by-step description of how she'll do the work. She extends an invitation to review the plan with Charles after he's had a chance to review it.

Step two is to make any required changes to your plan. Work with your micromanaging coworker until this person is satisfied that your plan is workable and detailed enough that you'll accomplish what needs to be done. How you proceed with this step will depend on if an agreement is reached or if an agreement isn't reached upon presentation of your action plan.

If agreement is reached

If agreement is reached, you can move forward with your work.

If agreement isn't reached

If agreement isn't reached, you need to make the changes necessary to gain agreement. You may want to ask how your coworker measures success or what the person's expectations are, and then incorporate that input into your plan. Again, move ahead with your work only once you achieve agreement on the what, how, and when details of your work.

A fter reviewing Amelia's plan, Charles has some concerns. The two meet to discuss the plan and make some changes. Amelia feels it's sufficient to generate a computer model of the new device. However, Charles would prefer it if she developed a working prototype. Even though she thinks this is unnecessary, it won't take that much time and will appease Charles. She also agrees to add details about how the prototype will be used, when, and by whom. Once these changes are made, Charles agrees the plan is sufficient.

Reflect

Why do think it might be beneficial to reach agreement with a micromanaging coworker before you begin working?

Step three is to be dependable. Conduct the work as agreed – essentially, do what you've said you'd do. This will help you to build a trusting relationship with your micromanaging coworker.

Always fulfill the commitments you made in your plan of action. Failing to do so will ruin your efforts to build the micromanager's trust in you.

When the micromanager trusts you, the person will likely interfere less, and feel less of a need to try to control everything you do.

N ow that Amelia is completing her work, she's taking care to stick to the plan that her and Charles agreed to. And she notices that Charles is not looking over her shoulder as often as he used to. She figures there's merit in changing her work habits to suit Charles's micromanaging ways. She's able to get her work done with minimal interruption from Charles, and she's no longer frustrated.

Step four of the process for appropriately dealing with micromanagers is to update the micromanager frequently. Providing frequent progress reports – perhaps even daily – satisfies a micromanager's "need to know" and reduces the number of times the micromanager comes to you for updates. This helps control and minimize the interruptions, which provides the benefit of improved overall productivity.

Amelia is about to leave work for the day. She's recently made it a habit to drop by Charles's office at the end of each workday to tell him what's going on with her work. She has found this to be an effective way of keeping Charles from interrupting her.

By following the four-step process, Amelia has found that Charles is micromanaging her less. She's getting more done and isn't as frustrated as she was the last time she worked with him. Amelia intends to use this process each time she needs to work with Charles. She believes that being dependable and working to accommodate Charles will help build his confidence in her. And their working relationship will continue to improve, allowing her to be more productive and less stressed.

C onsistently following this four-step procedure will help you build a relationship based on trust. The micromanager will notice that you're dependable and will have confidence in your abilities. In turn, this should minimize the micromanaging you're subjected to.

If this doesn't work, you may need to seek outside help. Your manager or supervisor is probably the most appropriate person to start with. Your immediate superiors are most likely to be familiar with the circumstances and individuals involved. You also want to avoid upsetting the chain of command.

If necessary, you can consider other potential sources of help outside your department:

- human resources
- the micromanager's supervisor or manager, if different from yours, and
- the company's employee assistance program, if it has one

Before seeking help, compile your evidence. Make sure you have proof that the micromanager's behavior is negatively impacting your performance. If applicable and available, you can also include information about how the micromanager's behavior is negatively impacting project or team efforts. Evidence gives weight to your argument and provides a better basis for action – you want to avoid being seen as pointing fingers and passing blame.

Micromanagers can be difficult to work with, and they aren't likely to change much, if at all. Consistently using a four-step process will help build the micromanager's confidence in you. With confidence will come trust in your ability, and the micromanager is likely to back off and let you work more independently.

The steps of the process are to lay out your plan of action ahead of time to the micromanager, make any required changes to your plan, be dependable, and update the micromanager frequently. Learning to deal with the micromanagers you encounter at work will reduce the negative impact they have on you.

60

Dealing with Micromanagers

Once you're comfortable in understanding the steps to deal with a micromanaging coworker, you'll be better equipped to put them into action. In turn, you'll be able to work more independently, keep reporting requirements reasonable, and improve your productivity.

Building a good working relationship with a micromanager requires you to establish trust and build the coworker's confidence in your abilities. Consistently following the four-step process for dealing with micromanagers can help you do this.

J asper and Caroline are working together on a project to create an in-house certification study guide. Jasper knows that Caroline tends to micromanage her coworkers. He decides to be proactive and change his approach to suit her needs and hopefully lessen her micromanagement of him. Before doing any project work, Jasper creates a detailed plan of what he'll do, and how and when he'll do it.

Jasper has finished his plan and is about to present it to Caroline for her review. Follow along as Jasper talks to Caroline about his plan.

Jasper: Caroline, I've outlined my contributions to this project and I'd like you to take a look before I start working. Since my work will impact yours, I thought it would be a good idea for us to be on the same page.

Caroline: Great, Jasper. Let's have a look. Your work spans the entire project.

Jasper: Yes. I'm in charge of creating the style sheet, editing, assuring quality, and ensuring final acceptance of the study guide. I've also included details of what I'll do, how, and when for each of my project tasks. Can you think of anything I missed, or do you have any input to improve on my plan?

Caroline: Well, I think you'd be better off doing a complete editorial review, instead of doing a section at a time. That way, you can catch any contradictions from section to section.

Working with Difficult People

Jasper: You mean wait until the study guide is written and then do one editorial review instead of smaller reviews as the guide is completed? Sure, I can do that. Anything else?

Caroline: No, the rest looks good to me. I can't wait to see how things progress.

Jasper: Ok, so I'll make that change and add the necessary details. Once I'm done, I'll e-mail you a finalized copy of the plan. Thanks for your input, Caroline.

Knowing that micromanagers need information, Jasper provides frequent updates on his progress. And knowing that Caroline will be watching him closely, Jasper is careful to follow the plan exactly.

Caroline has even complimented him on his attention to detail and ability to deliver. He knows this will help build Caroline's trust and confidence in him.

Jasper sends Caroline updates whenever an established milestone is reached. But he also e-mails Caroline daily updates, just to keep her well informed.

Practice: Deal with a Micromanager

Some time has passed since you and Sara agreed to your plan of action. Since then, you've been doing your best to stick to the plan. Sara checks in with you regularly.

As you moved through the four-step process with Sara, she responded more positively when you provided details and information freely and did what you said you would. Putting in the extra effort to accommodate her needs will alleviate her micromanaging and, in the end, will allow you to be more productive.

www.ingramcontent.com/pod-product-compliance
Lightning Source LLC
Chambersburg PA
CBHW021813170526
45157CB00007B/2577